Counselling for Family Problems

Counselling in Practice

Series editor: Windy Dryden
Associate editor: E. Thomas Dowd

Counselling in Practice is a series of books developed especially for counsellors and students of counselling which provides practical, accessible guidelines for dealing with clients with specific, but very common, problems.

Counselling for Family Problems

Eddy Street

SAGE Publications
London • Thousand Oaks • New Delhi

SAGE Publications Ltd
6 Bonhill Street
London EC2A 4PU

SAGE Publications Ltd
2455 Teller Road
Thousand Oaks, California 91320

SAGE Publications India Pvt Ltd
32, M-Block Market
Greater Kailash – I
New Delhi 110 048

British Library Cataloguing in Publication Data

Street, Eddy
  Counselling for Family Problems. –
  (Counselling in Practice)
  I. Title II. Series
  362.82

  ISBN 0–8039–8854–0
  ISBN 0–8039–8855–9 (pbk)

Library of Congress catalog card number 94-065455

Typeset by Mayhew Typesetting, Rhayader, Powys
Printed in Great Britain by Biddles Ltd, Guildford, Surrey

Contents

For Jenny, Tesni, Joe, and of course, Anna

Acknowledgements

There are very many people who, over the years, in one way or another have made contributions to my thinking about working with families. I have enjoyed interacting with them all as a student, a teacher, a colleague, a giver and a taker. Special mention needs to be made of Andy Treacher and Paul O'Reilly for their long-term support and friendship. Many thanks to Mark Rivett and Jim Wilson for their enthusiastic attitude to inquiry.

The practical tasks of writing this relatively short book have seemed enormous. I would like to thank Windy Dryden for his continued faith and encouragement. Many thanks to my wife, Anna, who acted as everything from a walking dictionary to philosophical debater as well as providing copious tea and comfort. Thanks are especially due to Anne Flower whose efficient typing and administrative skills, blended with her warmth, good humour and enthusiastic approach to this project, have not only been helpful but positively sustaining.

Preface

In the writing of this book I had three types of reader in mind. Those professionals who, in the course of their work, need to deal with families; individuals who are beginning the process of training in systemic work with families; and experienced practitioners who feel in need of some refreshment. What has been interesting in trying to meet these needs has been watching my own thoughts and ideas change in the process of writing. I started writing the middle sections, then wrote some of the introductory chapters, changed the middle, thought about the conclusion, changed the introduction and eventually 'discovered' the conclusion. Consequently my original ideas about the subject are different at the end of writing from what they were at the beginning. This is the way it should be, and hopefully this process of change and discovery will continue. I trust that this process is transmitted to the readers.

Chapter 1 provides an introduction to the systemic context of human development and the stresses of life faced by individuals and families. Chapter 2 outlines some concepts for considering the internal workings of family life. An overview of the model of change utilized in the book is presented in Chapter 3. Chapter 4 discusses the skills necessary initially to meet with a family in a counselling context and Chapter 5 follows on with a consideration of those skills necessary to establish a systemic view of the problem and set the scene for counselling. Some basic counselling intervention skills are outlined in Chapter 6, together with some specific interventive approaches. Chapter 7 takes on the theme of dealing with problem solving strategies which can be used by counsellor and family alike. Chapter 8 presents a series of approaches by which the counsellor and the family, separately and together, can monitor and review how counselling is progressing. The final chapter returns to the issues of a model of change and presents some general ideas about change in the family counselling context. The most obvious way to read the text is from Chapter 1 through to Chapter 9. However Chapters 1 and 2 form a unity on theoretical issues about families as systems; Chapters 3 and 9 are linked together as they deal with change concepts as applied to families, and Chapters 4–8 offer the practical material. For those who wish, a different ordering of chapters is possible based on these groupings.

Finally, there are many case examples offered in this book and some extended dialogue. All these examples are fictitious in that I made them up, but even though they derive from my imagination, I have in some way met all the families and all the situations contained in this book. It is from this experience that I have created these individuals and family contexts. I apologize to anyone who feels that I have too closely represented their own or a client's situation. It is in no way intended to breach confidentiality. There are, after all, millions of ways of being an individual but the psychological nature of human suffering is universal.

Eddy Street
Cardiff

1

Systems and Development: the Context for Understanding Family Problems

> But wishes breed not, neither
> Can we fend off rock arrival
>
> Dylan Thomas

Introduction

What is a family problem? Perhaps it would be quicker to ask what is not a family problem. Somebody falls off a chair in the kitchen and breaks a leg. Depending on the somebody, different things will happen. If it is a young child, the mother (usually) will take the child to the hospital, the father (or perhaps the grandparents) will be called to the home to look after the other children, someone (again usually mother) will need to alter her schedule to look after the child because he cannot go to school and so on. If it is a wife and mother who breaks her leg, the father may have to remain home from work to look after the children. This might not help the financial situation of the family so they cannot have their planned holiday and the children may start complaining as they are fed up of chips and beans for tea. Should this accident happen to an elderly man, it may result in him becoming more frail, necessitating an adult child (again usually a woman) doing his weekly shopping and 'popping in' more often, which may stop her from taking her night class which . . . etc., etc. Every type of problem has a relationship element. One person in a family cannot experience a difficulty without it having some effect on other family members. We are all linked in this way. Some difficulties appear as a part of the relationships themselves, for example, divorce, parenting problems, whereas other difficulties seem to occur because of unexpected events, for example, illness, handicap, accidents. Also just being young or old, having a job or not having a job, being black, having no money, all bring their difficulties. Whatever the origin of the problem, in order to deal with it effectively some change will need to occur within the family.

To appreciate how families make these changes, it is important to understand the functioning of the family as a system and to place this within the context of developmental processes.

Systems and human beings

Families, in whatever way they are constituted, are part of the natural world and it is not possible to conceive of the functioning of the natural world without thinking in terms of systems. This is regardless of whether one takes a tropical rain forest, a troupe of gibbons in Africa or a Welsh country hillside. The latter can be used to provide an example of how a natural system operates; on a Welsh hillside, the flora and fauna maintain each other in a form of balance; a hot summer occurs, insects increase, which brings more birds to the hillside looking for food, their presence destroys certain plants, which makes it less of a favourable habitat for the insects, which reduces the number of birds in the area, which allows the plants to reassert themselves and so it goes on. The characteristics of naturally occurring systems are outlined below.

Properties of open systems occurring in the natural world
1   A system is composed of inter-related parts, all of which combine to influence its total functioning.
2   A system functions by means of the patterns of connections between the parts.
3   The connections between the parts are established by means of information exchange. The constitution of 'information' will vary depending on the nature of the system.
4   As systems are composed of patterns of connections, it is arbitrary to decide where any open system begins and ends.
5   The system utilizes the information that passes between constituent parts to maintain itself in balance. A change in one element of information will result in a change elsewhere in the system so that functioning is maintained. This is known as **circular causality** or **circularity** and describes the process of feedback in the system.
6   A system cannot be independently observed. The process of observation creates a connection, which by creating information creates a new system. This is 'recognized' by the 'feedback' mechanism outlined in 5.

The family as a naturally occurring open system can be viewed in this light as càn other human groups and organizations. The focus of interest is on the pattern of connections between one individual and another, with individual characteristics being seen as the behaviour illustrating the connection rather than something located within the individual. Indeed it is more accurate to describe individuals as 'showing' certain behaviour rather than describing them as 'being' a particular type of person. Therefore, to say that a man is 'possessive' does not capture the sense of all the interactions around him at that particular time, or the viewpoint of the observer. It is more accurate to report that when certain interactions occur the man, from a particular point of view, is seen as displaying 'possessive type' behaviour. Human action and activity is therefore embedded within the connections, the interactions, between people. Any action is a response to the interactions within the system which, of course, are happening continually. So how one family member behaves is a direct response to the interactions of other family members whether those interactions are directed towards that individual or merely observed by that individual. 'Information exchange', the fuel of interaction of human systems, is what we know as communication. To be human is to be involved in communication; Birdwhistell (1959) in fact argued that it is erroneous to consider that individuals communicate for what they do is become a part of communication. Individuals are therefore part of the communication system we call the family and as Crook (1980) points out, to be involved in a communicating system is at the core of human identity as identity evolves socially. Our conception of a person requires that an individual displays self-awareness and also has the capacity to say what he or she is doing. Clearly a necessary condition for having the concept of oneself as a person is that other people should also recognize one as being a person. For this to happen a group of people must be able to know that each one of them has, at least, an idea as to what he or she is doing and can communicate it to others. As so much of our personal, private view of ourselves evolves out of our communication within our families, their interactions play the crucial central role in the view we have of who we are.

Curiously, as Bateson (1973) notes, even though humans are a part of groups and cultures which are systemic and are embedded in biological and ecological systems, there is a twist in the systemic nature of the individual person whereby consciousness is almost of necessity blinded to the systemic nature of human beings. Even though we are an element of interacting systems we somehow forget it. This occurs because every behaviour is at one and the same time both an expression of the person and a communication to others (Watzlawick et al., 1974). To emphasize one to the neglect of the other is to lose our essential systemic nature and for us as individuals there is a strong tendency to experience our communications solely as expressions of the self. We emphasize the 'What I do' to the neglect of 'This is my contribution to what We do'.

Another reason humans lose an overall conception of their systemic nature is that they need to formulate action ahead of events; they need to create strategies and tactics prior to being involved in situations of informational complexity. To achieve this a reflexive withdrawal from ongoing events is needed. The individual then focuses on a self-consciousness rather than the consciousness of the moment where the ongoing activities of others will have important influences on the interactive process. This allows the person to work out what he or she is going to do but the 'time out' period results in the loss of awareness of how the system is operating. The degree to which any individual indulges in an overly focused view of his or her own particular conception of events in the system will determine the extent to which that person is removed from appreciating his or her position within the functioning system. Within families this happens continually as family members focus on 'this is what I need', or 'this is what others do to me', rather than considering the process of interaction for the family as a whole.

Individuals and families therefore have the ability to understand the social interactive nature of themselves but unfortunately this understanding which requires the individual to subsume his or her identity within that of the system does not occur, particularly at times when problems arise.

Subsystems

As system boundaries are only arbitrary, there are systems within systems; the family is a subsystem of a community and within the family itself there will be component systems.

Each family member will be involved with other members differently.These different combinations being subsystems are made of the interactions of particular sets of individuals, mother, father, siblings, child–parent, grandparents and parents etc. The boundaries around such subsystems are arbitary but sometimes they have a functional value in that they circumscribe a particular set of tasks for those individuals within that subsystem. For example, there clearly are a number of particular tasks of parenting that need to be performed by mature adults (the parents) rather than by, say, siblings; this subsystem has been termed the executive subsystem because of its role in leading family direction (Minuchin, 1974). Different families will have different individuals operating within their varying subsystems and within each family and each subsystem it is possible to describe particular sets of circumstances where individuals behave differently. These are known as contexts.

Contexts

A context is a recognizable pattern of ideas or events created by family members which constructs a set of expectations thereby providing meaning to those events. Contexts vary according to the expectations one has about how they should operate. For example, if one walks unexpectedly into a doctor's waiting room and sees people dancing, wearing paper hats, it would be confusing until one sees a sign 'Staff Party – Tonight'. Context is not defined by the physical setting but by the expectation of how individuals should behave in that setting at that time. In terms of relationships, for example, a woman may be used to her husband complaining about his workmates. She recognizes this communication and knows from past experience that if she listens and agrees they both feel satisfied. However, when the same couple talk about decorating their bedroom both may recognize that in this context they can each have their say and disagree. Their beliefs about the interactions of the other serve to set their expectations which leads to their actual behaviour. Families that function adequately are able to recognize a greater number of contexts within their overall interaction and are able to adapt and change these contexts as the situation demands. Families experiencing problems struggle to recognize and change the appropriate context as their beliefs and expectations of the situation do not help them. Families that are dysfunctional tend to be more rigid in the number of contexts they recognize and hence the way they behave. In the above example, a rigid pattern would be present in the relationship if, when talking about the decorating, both husband and wife had some expectations that the husband will talk and the wife will agree – behaviour relevant to one context but not necessarily to the other.

Thinking systemically

The challenge for us as human beings is therefore to understand our place and role within the families, groups, cultures and environments we inhabit. To do this we need to explore our beliefs and the meanings that we construct to explain the world around us. The meanings individuals attribute to their activity comprise the 'sociogrammar' of human activity (Crook, 1980), and this way of organizing our understanding requires to be brought into awareness. We therefore need to be able to think systemically in order to appreciate our own functioning and this is important not just for how we as individuals function in the world, but particularly in terms of the endeavour we are embarked on here, namely being a helper to a family. But to start to think about the family as a system the would-be family counsellor needs to begin with an appreciation of those systemic features that are present in the counselling room. Hopefully as this book unfolds the reader will be helped to operationalize systemic thinking, and to begin to understand that in families human development should be considered first.

Family life cycle and development

There are numerous theories and models of human development which tend to fall into one of three broad categories:

1   The psychodynamic model, which emphasizes the modification of needs, drives and affect through life.
2   The social learning model, which, resting on behavioural conceptions, bases the shaping of behaviour on social reinforcement.
3   The organic model, which is based on the sequential unfolding of abilities and characteristics that are in some way present from birth.

Events that, according to these models, indicate developmental progress are presented as linear, unidirectional and concentrate very much on the individual, on his or her path from birth to death. To describe movement in the family system in a similar, linear fashion is not so helpful. A model of family systems development has to address a number of issues that focus primarily on maintaining the perspective of individuals changing through time, through natural maturational processes while considering the systemic nature of family life, the way it is linked to its social environment and the social evolution of identity by these processes.

One of the initial requirements of such a systems view is to consider the nature of change that occurs in families as the outcome of simple developmental pressures. Terkelsen (1980) poses a three-level model of such changes; at the basic level are those relatively short behavioural sequences that characterize a family's day-to-day functions; some elements of these sequences may change depending on daily conditions. At the next level is 'first order change', where individuals alter their own behaviour to accommodate their developing mastery of their situation. The uppermost layer involves 'second order change', which refers to the family systems adaptation to individual changes which results in an alteration of meaning within the system and thus new behavioural sequences are generated. Obviously one form of change feeds into the next in a circular fashion. Let us return to our initial example of the broken leg, focusing on it occurring in a young child. Because of the broken leg the child may not be able to walk home from school and convenience dictates that the father pick up the child from school. This is a simple change of structure in that a relatively short sequence is altered. A first order change may then occur as the mother appreciates that she no longer needs to be so mindful of simple parenting tasks as her husband is equally capable. The change of awareness and perception of herself is very much an individual developmental issue, but in order for the family to deal with this change a second order adaptation is required. The father now has to alter more of his behaviour to accommodate to his wife's new perception and the meaning of being a parent in the family will change as it involves more joint activity from the couple. Similarly, there will be changes in how all the children view their parents and their understanding of what they expect from their parents and themselves will change. In other words, the meaning of the child–parent relationship will alter – and all because someone broke a leg.

This example points to the fact that changes occurring within each individual and each subsystem will affect second order changes that will, in turn, reverberate in the whole system producing a kaleidoscopic rearrangement of parts. The example also illustrates Hoffman's (1989) assertion that development is not a continuous process but one characterized by transformations, second order changes and the sudden appearance of functionally organized patterns that simply did not exist before. The timing and nature of developmental shifts cannot be predicted, though predictions can be made about the issues and the direction of organization that will take place. So, for example, we could not have foreseen that the unexpected broken leg of a 10-year-old boy would have resulted in a successful re-negotiation of parenting within the context of gender roles but we could have predicted that roughly within a particular time frame gender roles and parenting older children would become an issue that would set tasks for this family. This example, however, lacks another important dimension, namely the interaction of the nuclear family with the grandparents, for how this older generation was involved in the young family may also now change. They may for instance be required less for child care and will face anew the question of what to do with their time. The resultant changes faced by the older members are different from those faced by the younger adults and different again from those the children have to deal with. Clearly then, adopting multigenerational perspective demonstrates that one event can have many repercussions throughout the family. These repercussions cannot be described according to a 'unified' task for each generation is confronted by different issues, many of which reflect contemporary beliefs about people of that particular generation. Thus, for example, beliefs about the changing role of women will impact on the generations differentially. Hence if we limit descriptions of development to one individual or one subsystem we severely curtail our appreciation of the complexity of life. The one event, however, can, by framing a new context, create tasks for each generation which are reciprocally linked to the tasks of another generation.

History and development

In their discussion of multigenerational development within families, Carter and McGoldrick (1989) note that although family processes are not linear, they do exist in the linear dimension of time. As the family move forward through time they have to deal with pressures that come from the predictable course of development (**developmental stresses**) together with the unpredictable stresses of chronic illness, untimely death, accident, divorce and remarriage. They contrast this to historical stresses in the system (**transgenerational stresses**), including patterns of relating and functioning that are transmitted down the generations of a family (Bowen, 1978). These stressors include all the family attitudes, taboos, expectations, labels and loaded issues with which each member grows up and different cultures and subcultures will experience a different set of these 'norms'. Although normative change in any culture is to some degree stressful, when developmental stresses intersect with transgenerational stress, there is a massive increase of anxiety in the system and dysfunction can result. Our 'broken leg' family would have met considerably more problems if as well as the developmental stresses the strong transgenerational messages were that women alone should look after the children. We can see from this that although a developmental model provides a framework for considering the predictable elements of family life, idiosyncratic histories and serendipitous events will produce the specific development for each family.

A family systems model

A model for considering the family life cycle is presented in chart form in Table 1.1 and immediately it is important to say that this is inadequate to meet the needs of the situation. This is simply because one cannot convey the complexity of multigenerational perplexity in such a form. The method that has been chosen to highlight the stages of family life begins with the individual. This is because, as Combrinck-Graham (1985) notes, individual life cycles may be conceptualized as the threads from which the family context is woven, changes in the individual threads being reflected in the appearance and shape of the family context. It would not be correct in using this model to name the phases, for the naming process tends to limit the description and observation to only an individual or a small subsystem. The name would focus observations on the issues between spouses or between parents and one child, without considering the family as a whole. 'Names' are only used on the chart as a means of orientating the reader. It should also be noted that convention dictates that the age of the oldest child is the one used to mark the phases for parenting adults. The chart, for sake of space, also neglects to include a column for 'grandparent tasks', for these are included in the later parental tasks – the existence of a grandparent column would have served to maintain a multigenerational perspective. The chart also seems to 'wither' and become less complex as the individual becomes older and this is an impression given by the vertical nature of the chart. Of course, as time passes the older individual is part of a family with younger individuals and hence the chart should be larger and should seem to move diagonally from right to left as the elderly die and new children are born.

The chart focuses on the notion of a task. These are issues that have to be dealt with in order that the next set of issues on the path of development can be approached. Tasks by their very nature are relationship-bound and involve interaction with other family members and by the generational effect referred to above the tasks of one generation influence and are related to the tasks of another generation. Thus, for example, an individual requires some degree of personal autonomy to separate from parents and the parents need to be able to allow this to happen. Hence the task for the individual of separating becomes a foundation for the task of forming extrafamilial relationships and the task for the parents of allowing separation underpins the marital tasks that follow after the children have left home. Clearly the 'solution' of any task is important for future development but what is of equal importance is the process of solving itself. Indeed development,

Table 1.1 *Family life cycle*

Phase and tasks for individual	Phase of parents	Parenting tasks	Marital tasks
1 Babyhood: Discovery of own body. Self–other discrimination. Development of basic trust	Young adulthood	Considerable constancy of caring needed. Accept extreme dependence. Begin to accept baby as a person	Maintain links of family and outside world. Support for carer. Acceptance of third individual. Redefinition of closeness
2 Toddlers: Learning to walk and ability to move away from caring adult. Cope with ability to hurt loved ones. (Limitation of acceptable behaviour explored.) Accept pain and shame and doubt. Begin to discover gender identity	Young adulthood	Careful mangement of distance. Sensitivity to self-esteem. Accept and help define personal characteristics. Accept play. Provide appropriate tasks to develop skills. Begin to negotiate agreed discipline philosophy	Maintenance of support for carer
3 Pre-school: Learning about three-person relationships. Balancing feelings of belonging and being 'outside'. Begin to learn values and rules	Young adulthood	Accept child's gender identity. Establish clear generational and role boundaries. Give clear rules and values	Confirm context of marital relationship within context of clarifying generational boundaries
4 Early school years: Accept care from adult other that parents. Begin separating from parents. Share caring adult with classmates. Enjoy and use peers	Early mid-life	Accept ability to separate and allow closeness to peers and to teachers. Encourage interests, even when different from the family. Balance children's and parents' outside interests	Negotiate end of childbearing phase. Deal with change in maternal role. Renegotiate separateness and togetherness. Redefining of commitment to the marriage
5 Adolescence: Find ways to accept and enjoy sexuality first in fantasy then by identifying potential partners and exploring relationships with them. Exploring and then developing identity characteristics of the self. Differentiate from parents	Mid-life	Tolerate re-emergence of early tendencies. Accept intense mixture of progressive and regressive trends. Acceptance of impending adulthood of offspring	Re-establish the couple as an entity separate from the family. Support during periods of crisis and doubt that mid-life brings

6 Young adulthood: Establish separate lifestyle and domicile. Find adult social roles. Set up enduring relationships and loves. Negotiate with society about capabilities	Mid-life	Accept distance of young adult offspring. Accept offspring as peers	Find satisfactory marriage without children. Maintain separate and mutual interests
7 Courtship and marriage: Balancing the merging process of loving with the maintenance of the separate identity. Begin to negotiate life together	Mid-life	Begin to manage in-law status	Re-evaluation of marital pair as parents. Review notion of marriage
8 Young adulthood: Parenting phase. Accept dependency of self and others. Accept roles that family life brings. Rely on the help of others including extended family	Late mid-life	Grandparent phase. Accept new need for offspring to be close as adults. Provide additional adults for children to identify with	Preparation for closeness that retirement will bring
9 Early mid-life: Reappraisal of own power and status. Creation of self roles other than sex and work roles. Awareness of mortality	Retirement	Accept ending of parental tasks	Accept changing nature of dependency and of the sexual relationship
10 Late mid-life: Acceptance of achievements and plateau of achievements. Continuing development of spiritual and cultural interests. Accept dependency of parents and future loss	Old age		Accept future loss of partner
11 Retirement: Acceptance of loss of work roles. Evaluation of life successes and failures			
12 Old age: Acceptance of dependency. Acceptance of infirmity and death			

both for the individual and family, can best be conceived of as the continual process of solving tasks that human life and endeavour set. As Watzlawick et al. (1974) have noted, there is no such thing as a problem-free life and our idea of who we are is gained from the manner in which we confront and live through life's problems and tasks, all of which are interactionally bound. Indeed in a consideration of an individual in the system it can seen that a person's experience is at its essence a social phenomenon as it is contained within reciprocal interaction. The person is constructing a self by creating meaning and by making initiatives within that framework of meaning, which adapts to the evolving conditions and tasks of life. As this is a responsive process, a person's experience of self is not held constant through life. It changes as circumstances change.

From Table 1.1 it can be seen that the family system appears to oscillate between periods of family closeness and periods when individuals are more distant and disengaged. Combrinck-Graham (1985) identifies the close periods as 'centripetal' to indicate the predominance of forces in the family system that hold the family together and the distant periods as 'centrifugal', as the forces predominantly pull the family members out. The centripetal periods being the birth/child-bearing periods when grandparents may be required to help with child care and the centrifugal periods when a child is adolescent and the parents are undergoing the re-evaluation common in mid-life. A family will undergo three oscillations during an individual's average expected lifetime: the birth and adolescence of X, the birth and adolescence of X's children and then the birth and adolescences of X's grandchildren. Repeating the experience provides the individual and couples with opportunities for reworking through particular issues. Life's developments therefore provide events that encourage both the primacy of relationships and then alternatively the self-expression of individuality; these oscillations offer a practice ground for experiencing intimacy and self-actualization at different levels of maturity and through different tasks in the context of the family environment.

Transitions
Stress in the family's development is at its highest level as the family move from one phase of life to another. This period of movement is known as a *transition*. The stress is induced as second order change is required, in which new meaning and structure are needed in order successfully to adapt to the change. Transitions are not necessarily stressful nor are they confined to the categories of

phases one adopts to cover the life cycle. Some transitions become particularly problematic because other external stressors impinge on the family's coping mechanism. Many of the unpredictable events of life also demand changes which require a transition to a different means of functioning, thus the birth of a handicapped child, achieving single parent status, chronic illness etc., all will involve family changes to a considerable extent. It is useful to conceive of a transition being the period of instability while the family change from state A to state B; therefore a transitional period should retrospectively be of a definable time. Some families, because of their history, deal with particular transitions very well and not so well with others. Where felt anxiety, doubt and uncertainty are experienced, then one can consider there being a *transitional crisis*. Families differ in the extent to which they are adaptable (Olsen et al., 1988) and hence deal with transitions, but this characteristic is affected by the context of the moment.

One can therefore use this model of the family life cycle rapidly to ascertain the possible transition the family is facing and the nature of the tasks they need to perform in order to achieve a level of functioning which is stabilizing and meets the intimacy and self-actualizing needs of its members. We cannot predict the unexpected, this framework, however, does provide a good means of appreciating how a family may deal with such events in terms of their developmental context.

Dealing with stress

The vagaries of life and the perpetual changing nature of the world we inhabit throw up expected and unexpected events which we have to deal with. Families display a wide range of adaptations to similar events. For example, Byrne et al. (1988) have produced evidence to demonstrate that some families experience considerable stress on having a child with Down's Syndrome, while others have found ways of adapting so that they are not under undue stress, with the child being viewed positively. Clearly nothing can be labelled as stressful unless it is perceived as such by family members. Stress is only identified as such when individuals believe that any given situation will place demands on themselves that will tax or exceed the resources available to them (Lazarus, 1990). Stress is not equivalent to the triggering event, or the circumstances surrounding that event, nor is it something that resides within an individual; stress is the result of an interaction between an individual or family and the circumstances in which they find themselves. Stress is therefore contextual.

A family cope and adapt to a situation when they use their thoughts and behaviour to manage the internal and external demands of the situation perceived as stressful. Adaptation to stress therefore emphasizes what the family think and do to deal effectively with the circumstances they face. Active adaptation or coping has two major functions: to regulate or reduce stressful emotions (emotion-focused coping) and to alter the troubling situation by behaving in a way that makes some difference (problem-focused coping). Research suggests that both types of coping are used together (Folkman and Lazarus, 1980, 1985) and some strategies may serve both functions. For example, a man experiencing difficulties with his step-daughter may tell a friend in a similar situation about this. In doing so he 'lets off steam' and feels better about it as a consequence – an emotion-focused strategy. However, in the course of the conversation the friend may in recounting his own experience implicitly make a practical suggestion that is subsequently followed – a problem-focused strategy. Again research by Folkman and Lazarus (1985) suggests that a good problem-focused coping strategy is one that places an emphasis on understanding and being able to analyse the particular situation. Such an approach has been found to be associated with lower levels of distress, for example, amongst families dealing with a handicapped child (Knussen and Sloper, 1992). How families adapt to stressful situations is therefore influenced by their appraisal of the demands of the tasks placed before them and the resources they have at their disposal. Folkman (1984) has broadly categorized the resources that families require in order to adapt to stress, as follows:

• Material – income, housing, belongings, car ownership and other variables associated with employment status and socio-economic class.
• Physical – personal health, strength, fitness mobility.
• Psychological – values, beliefs, attitudes, previous experience.
• Social – practical and emotional social support within the family and in the wider community.

Any counselling help aimed at a family should be focused on the psychological and social resources so that these can then be used to maximize the material and physical resources available. These resources will obviously vary depending on the stage of the life cycle, as well as material and physical factors including class and ethnicity.

As families move through time, their appraisal of stress changes, as does the coping strategies they apply. Also strategies that are useful at one point in time may be quite unhelpful at another. Similarly within families the manner in which different individuals appraise stress will vary and this difference will in itself prove stressful. If the stress remains and repeated efforts to deal with it fail, then the family's health and well-being will be negatively affected and their ability to deal with other stresses seriously compromised. Alternatively if a stressful situation is satisfactorily resolved it can leave the family stronger and happier, with confidence in their ability to deal with the future as their resources have been strengthened in demonstrating adaptations to the situation. As life is constantly producing stressful situations, the potential positive outcomes of dealing with them adequately should not be forgotten.

Lewis (1986) has proposed a continuum of family approaches to dealing with stressful events. Ideally a family should approach any situation in a flexible manner but when this breaks down a dominant–submissive interactive pattern is applied. Should this pattern fail then a family's interaction will become more conflicted, ultimately becoming chaotic. Typically families operate within a particular range of this continuum.

In order to prevent potentially stressful events from distorting the developmental process, particularly in children, Rutter (1987) suggests that protective mechanisms are established. Thus he emphasizes the importance of a sense of well-being or resilience developing in relation to the way in which a family appraise an event so that then they can help each other attach a constructive meaning to it and eventually incorporate it into their own conceptual system. So, for example, many of the effects originally thought to be due to damage caused by parental death are now seen as being linked to how the family members dealt with the experience at the time and how the child and adults aided each other in making sense of the family process. Rutter suggests there are four ways in which protective processes that encourage resilience can be set in motion.

1 The reduction of risk impact at times of family crisis or acute stress.
2 The reduction of negative chain reactions at times of family crisis or acute stress.
3 The establishment and maintenance of self-esteem and a sense of coping.
4 The opening of opportunities and the creation of choice.

These are all clearly aims for family counselling and they point directly to the importance of counselling's being seen as a beneficial adjunct to normative developmental processes.

2

Families in Operation

The world of the happy man is a different one from that of
the unhappy man.

Ludwig Wittgenstein

Families need to cope with the daily problems of living, to face up
to the challenges of development and provide for the emotional
needs of their members. These tasks have to be met in a way that
offers consistency and security amid the continually changing
nature of the situation in which the family find themselves. In
order to make sense of the multitude of interactions necessary to
meet these tasks a framework is required for understanding how a
family, as a system, organizes itself. The model to be proposed
here will rest on the notion of time frames for considering
interaction and the themes that encompass the challenges of family
development.

Operational features

Time frames and meaning
Within the field of family therapy counselling there are many
models each with different emphases and approaches to observing
and describing interaction; the most obvious common denominator
to these models is the concept that family behaviour is patterned
and thus time and again families repeat the same class of interaction. A corollary to this is the idea that 'symptom' behaviour is
related to or part of some of the interaction patterns. To describe
a pattern in its entirety for any given family or interpersonal
system is impossible because it requires the ability to observe and
define a highly complex and continuous stream of behavioural
sequences that are connected and persist over time. Despite this
difficulty, Breunlin and Schwartz (1986) propose a model that
examines the relationships of sequences within the entire pattern of

a family and is based on time frames. They identify four classes of sequences:

1   From seconds to hours.
2   A day to a week.
3   Several weeks to a year.
4   Time that spans at least one generation.

Some sequences are recursive in that they are repeating, with an element of themselves guaranteeing their repetition. Some sequences are non-recursive in that they involve sequences of behaviours that do not repeat over time. Within a given generation life cycle events such as births and marriages are non-recursive, that is, they do not repeat; on taking the wider frame of a generation, however, they may be recursive as families repeat the same pattern. As these sequences are interlocking, with one type of sequence linked to those that are of longer or shorter duration, at any one time a small interactive sequence may reflect the past, the present and be part of an anticipated future. An example of this would be as follows: a child disobeys his mother and she tells him off – a short sequence. But over the course of the day the child's behaviour becomes increasingly worse, when the father returns home his wife tells him the story of the day and the father admonishes the child. Over the course of a month the father becomes frustrated as he sees himself always telling the child off so he tells his wife she should deal with the problem and he withdraws; however, the problem continues, the mother becomes angry with the father, they argue and the father begins to admonish the child. This sequence may constantly repeat itself over its monthly cycle. The sequence may also find its elements intergenerationally in that the adults concerned both came from families with a man oscillating in his involvement with his children on a discipline theme and a woman struggling with children and having to insist on the involvement of a man.

Any problem is embedded in one or more interactional sequences. However, it does not follow that for every problem there are sequences from each of the time frames as different problems are contained in different time frames.

In seeking a resolution of a problem it will be necessary that the family agree on the meaning of the sequence so that the appropriate time frame can be discussed. Meaning is central to the interaction process in that when it is agreed it provides the context to enable individuals to coordinate their action, manage their relationship and hence deal with any problem that emerges. In a manner that builds on the time frames notion, Cronen and Pearce

(1985) link the different levels of meaning that are available to family members and suggest five levels which, as with the time frames, are shown to be interlocking. So that the reader appreciates the circularity of short to long and long to short, these levels of meaning are in the opposite order to the time frames above.

5 **Family myth** – includes general conceptions of how society, personal roles and family relationships work.
4 **Life script** – a person's conception of self in interaction.
3 **Relationship** – conception of how and on what terms two or more persons engage in interaction.
2 **Episode** – a short pattern of reciprocated interaction.
1 **Speech act** – verbal or non-verbal messages from one person.

Clearly with these levels of meaning family myths inform life scripts, which inform relationships etc., and episodes construct relationships which construct life scripts etc. The episode and speech act level of meaning are contained within the first here-and-now class of sequences though a speech act is not a sequence itself, it being just one event. Relationships and life scripts overlap into the second and third sequences of time, whereas family myths are contained within the generational time span sequences. These ideas allow outsiders, such as counsellors, on meeting a family to orientate themselves to the appropriate meaning 'level' or time frame of what is happening at any one time.

Themes and challenges

Human beings and the families they form have to deal with three essential tasks or challenges in social interaction that define who they perceive themselves to be. They need to establish who is involved in their interactions and in what way; they need to experience a sense of control and influence over what happens to themselves; and they also need to share the affective elements of those tasks with other individuals (Lewis, 1986).

A model which addresses these themes is the Family FIRO Model as expounded by Doherty and his colleages (Doherty and Colangelo, 1984). This model has been derived from Schutz's Fundamental Interpersonal Relations Orientation (FIRO) theory of group development (Schutz, 1966). It holds that three fundamental issues predominate in human relatedness: inclusion, control and intimacy, and these three issues determine the framework for understanding the types of interactions that occur within a family's life.

Inclusion
These are interactions that relate to membership, organization and bonding. There are three subcategories:

1   Structure – repetitive patterns that become routine. These patterns define the **boundaries** of the family as well as the boundaries of the family's subsystems. Amongst the most important patterns are those that define the **intergenerational boundaries** (that is, the way members of different generations interact with each other) and those that define the **executive subsystem** (that is, the system that is 'in charge', usually the parental couple).
2   Connectedness – the bonding interactions between family members. These interactions vary from individuals being so close they can think and feel for each other (enmeshed) to being very separate (disengaged). Individuals' sense of belonging derive from this.
3   Shared meaning – interactions associated with the family's sense of its special identity as a group. This involves the values the family members hold, the beliefs and ideas they share and the **family ideology** they espouse about how they operate in the world, reflecting the family's view of its own interactions in all domains.

Family inclusion defines who is in and out of the family and how its subsystems are composed and in defining this the roles individuals occupy are specified, as well as the connectedness of those individuals. Such definitions contribute to the shared meaning of the family, constituting the ideas they have about themselves. The shared meaning or family ideology is central in that it reflects the family's view of itself and therefore is both the window and the door for observing, understanding and joining the family.

Control
These are interactions that relate to responsibility, discipline, power, decision-making and influence. As conflict is inevitable in families, the struggle associated with it may be overt or covert. These conflicts often centre around particular content issues such as money. There are three major types of control interactions:

1   Dominating control – interactions in which a person attempts by confrontation to dictate, manipulate, coerce another person to undertake some behaviour. This of course can be appropriate, as in the disciplining of young children.

2   Reactive control – interactions in which a person, in response to a perceived request from another, resists, rebells, withdraws or disobeys. Here the person attempts to counteract the other's attempt to influence.

3   Collaborative control – these interactions include negotiations, compromises, giving and taking and generally attempting to work through conflict situations.

Control interactions occur in situations where family members perceive their needs as potentially competing and where they take steps to deal with this conflict by attempting to influence either overtly or covertly. It needs to be noted that men and women tend to use different mixtures of control interactions, which in itself can cause problems (see Perelberg and Miller, 1990).

The three types of control interactions are conceptually inter-related as facets of one interactional process, for as one member dominates, another may react. Similarly in any conflict situation the three types of interaction may be found and follow particular family patterns in terms of how they link to each other. Inclusion issues are quite often the outcome of control interactions. For example, marital role patterns represent the inclusive aspect of the relationship but marital bargaining over differences in role expectations is a matter of control processes. The collaborative category of control interactions offers the possibility of mutual sharing with an agreed balance of influence rather than the uni-laterality or reactivity of the other methods of dealing with power issues. It needs to be remembered that in families control issues are not always between equals. Parenting functions, for example, require a different set of interactions – indeed a flexible blend of parent–child interactions are necessary. Different blends would also be required for the sharing of a home with three generations, the care of an infirm elderly relative, caring for a chronically sick spouse etc.

Once individuals have struggled through conflict they are then available for intimate interaction which comprises the third and final theme and challenge.

Intimacy
These are interactions that relate to open self-disclosure and close personal exchanges. This involves the sharing of feelings, hopes, fears and vulnerabilities. For this to occur at high levels, a considerable degree of personal differentiation from the family of origin is necessary. True intimacy transcends family roles and involves 'I–Thou' relationships.

During intimate interactions, individuals relate to each other as unique human beings mutually sharing the variety of emotional experience they encounter and reaffirming the sense they have of their own identities. Intimacy implies interaction between peers in contrast to the more unilateral nurturing love of parents for young children or the affectionate distance of many couples in traditional marriages. But intimacy is not exclusively found between husbands and wives. It is capable of being found between any adults in the family though it does tend to be primarily found in dyadic interaction.

During intimate interaction meaning is not always present to inform action. As meaning evolves out of the mutual construction of interaction, it is possible to distinguish an area of family interactive life that is 'meaning-free' where people relate just as they are at that point in time and intimately share the existential moment. This area of family life has been called the 'open ground' (Welwood, 1983). When current and past fears impinge and the tasks of daily living present themselves, meaning and structure are created out of the open ground and we become distracted from our awareness of the moment. The constructed meaning can then become too dense and thick to allow for the changing nature of life to be encountered. We become rigid in our thinking and our action. There then is a need to allow this rigidity to dissolve back into the meaning-free open ground. In functioning relationships this is found in intimate interaction, for true intimacy implies 'meaning-free-ness', a place where we are free from the struggle of finding meaning. Intimate relationships therefore offer individuals the opportunity to recharge themselves and be able to deal with a world that requires meaning and structure. It should be noted, however, that it is possible for families to be quite an integrated, cohesive and functioning group without there being intimacy (Wynne, 1984). But when individuals and families experience a problem and seek help the therapeutic aim is to create interaction designed ultimately to establish the conditions for intimacy by offering the possibility of some 'open ground' in the counselling context.

The links between inclusion, control and intimacy

This framework for understanding themes is valuable in that it allows observers and families to be able to orientate themselves appropriately to the variety of issues that occur as a family live their lives. Of course family interactions are complex events and most will involve a blend of inclusion, control and intimacy dynamics. Unravelling the complexity of these interactions will be important in any work designed to help the family, especially as these patterns change to meet any life cycle transition or major ongoing stressful event. Major family change is almost always synonymous with altered patterns of family inclusion – birth, leaving home, marriage, divorce, death. As the one-time predictable interactive patterns require alteration, there are quite likely to be control struggles among family members who have different expectations about revised roles, who feel less connected and who perceive and understand events differently. These changes and conflicts will then have a knock-on effect on the intimacy encountered in the family and the emotional atmosphere for a time is likely to be one not conducive to openness. As the clarification of inclusion issues allows for a more appropriate context for control issues to be settled, this in turn creates an atmosphere where intimacy can be enjoyed. It is therefore adaptive for families challenged to create new interactive patterns to address issues in the order of inclusion, control and intimacy (Doherty et al., 1991). For example, a couple have their first child; their priority will be in their redefinition of the inclusion domain. Will there be a primary carer? Will someone work part-time? How will they view how they are connected to themselves and the child? How will they perceive of themselves as a family? To change adaptively they need to alter their patterns of interaction so that they construct a structure that works for them and this structure may be derived via particular control interactions with collaborative interactions obviously being more productive. Once the new structure meets the daily tasks of living in a satisfactory way for them, they will find their intimacy increases, particularly if they have dealt with control issues collaboratively.

Should a couple be having power struggles over money, be complaining they do not talk about their feelings any more and be considering whether to separate, the latter (inclusion) issue should be the first to be addressed as it will involve a commitment to deal with the control and intimacy issues. The finding of a solution to the possible separation may then establish collaborative interaction which in itself is the foundation for an atmosphere conducive to intimacy. This order does appear to be in reverse to what one would instinctively espouse, in that the intimacy is seen as being paramount. But for everyone the foundation of intimacy is trust that the other person is committed (inclusion) and trust that the other person will be fair when there is a conflict of interest (control). Perceived lack of commitment and fairness serve to prevent the experience of intimacy and clearly such undermining processes need to be ameliorated before individuals in families can have a sense of intimacy they desire.

Families in operation and schools of change

Individuals and families fail to make adaptive changes when there is a fear of psychological discomfort from perceived future choices. Also there is always ambivalence in human relationships and pain in the experience of that. Much of human action therefore consists of the attempt to achieve at least a gesture of balance in the face of the anguish and mixed blessings of living. All counsellors can work with the assumption that individuals seek clarity, poise and intimacy and the counselling process is aided by the tendency to self-righting that individuals in their contexts display. These unmistakable features of the therapeutic endeavour lie at the heart of most schools and models of counselling and therapy. Those models that address the systemic dimension in working with families emphasize different elements and they have approached the time frame and thematic dimensions differentially depending on their emphasis. This is due to the fact that inclusion themes are more obvious in the shorter time frames, control themes occur more readily in the medium term, whereas the longer sequences are clearly linked to intimacy issues. Thus Minuchin's structural therapy (Minuchin, 1974) emphasizes boundary, role patterns and connectedness within families in which short in-session interactions are addressed. Those models that emphasize control themes, such as strategic approaches (Haley, 1976), the earlier Milan approaches (Palazzoli et al., 1978), brief models (Watzlawick et al., 1974) and behavioural approaches (Jacobson and Margolin, 1979), emphasize intermediate time frames. In these approaches therapy consists of changing the family's role systems for mutual regulation either by overt steps (for example, teaching new behavioural strategies or eliciting new problem solving behaviour) or covert therapeutic moves (paradoxical prescriptions). Therapists with a focus on intimacy tend to be transgenerational in their consideration of time; the Family Systems Theory of Bowen (Bowen, 1978), Whitaker's Symbolic Experiential Model (Whitaker and Keith, 1981) and the Contextual Therapy of Boszormenyi-Nagyf (Boszormenyi-Nagy and Krasner, 1986) are approaches within this category, providing as they do goals for optimal individual and family functioning which involves dyadic intimacy outside of normative role patterns. The relationship of these schools to each other is displayed in Table 2.1.

Table 2.1 *Schools of family therapy and counselling*

Themes of family life			
Time frame sequences	Inclusion	Control	Intimacy
1 Short (up to hours)	Structural	↑	
2 Medium (up to a week)	↓	Behavioural	
3 Medium (up to a year)		Brief Strategic Milan	
			↑
4 Long (over one generation)		↓	Symbolic Experiential Contextual Transgenerational
			↓

The family counselling model being proposed here emphasizes the sense the family makes of itself and sees the process of change as occurring through their own action and thought. As we have seen, early therapists in this field focused their encounter on specific interaction sequences, but as Hoffman (1985) has pointed out, this involves the meanings of the observers predominating rather than those meanings constructed by the observed, that is, the family. It is the family and its functioning as revealed through its ideology that presents itself to the counsellor for help and this obviously needs to remain centre stage. This approach is therefore aimed to traverse time spans, meaning levels and themes in order to assist the family in realizing their own perspectives on these issues. It therefore attempts to reveal to individuals their systemic nature in operation within the humanistic tradition. This is not to say that other methods and approaches may not be useful. Indeed some approaches may be comprehensive in their execution by individual therapists and particular methods may be beneficial at particular times, but there is need for an approach which attempts to do justice to the range of family problems as the family themselves see it in that it deals with family context in terms of their own definition.

3

The Change Process in Family Counselling

> To be in the process of change is not an evil, any more than
> to be the product of change is a good.
>
> Marcus Aurelius

Change and 'new' information

In systemic terms human groups including families operate by the exchange of information and in systemic terms information can be ideas, feelings, behaviour and interactions. Families that have problems are repeatedly exchanging the same information in a way that is dissatisfying and non-functional for them; additionally the repeating nature of the information exchange is such that there is little chance of new information being generated. In other words, because things are stuck nothing different happens. Therefore the aim of the family counsellor is to assist the family in generating information to help form ideas, feelings, behaviours or interactions that are 'new' for them. However, it is unlikely that the 'newness' will mean that the information is completely novel or never experienced; it is likely that the new components will, in some senses, already be within the repertoire of the family and its members. The 'newness' refers to the novelty or difference of the information appearing in a particular family context. Once some difference is introduced, information is exchanged and a different interactive sequence becomes possible. The family can then move on and away from the problem that was causing them difficulty.

The human change process can vary depending on whether it is focused on the emotional, the cognitive or the behavioural elements of activity. Within family counselling, however, these three dimensions intertwine as an interactive change can be the product of a difference in thinking, feeling or doing for all these constitute 'information' within the family. A small difference in one part of the system can lead to a considerable change elsewhere. A difference that is noticed by the contributing individuals changes the context, thereby requiring the other individuals to determine how they will now behave. Hence a relatively minor change in one family member can, because of his or her position within the family, have considerable repercussions for how that family system will eventually operate. As the 'minor change' constitutes thinking, feeling or doing that is possible and may be already present, then the counselling task is to find a way of initiating that 'minor change' so that a different interactive sequence is unlocked.

Questioning the system

To help the family in the discovery of new information relevant to their particular problem, the counsellor simply asks questions. The questions she asks are about how individuals think, feel and behave and how groups of individuals interact. The counsellor *asks questions of the system* so that the information produced will reveal the way the family is interconnected and the means by which it, as a system, operates in its own circular fashion. As this information is generated the family are then provided with the opportunity of becoming aware of their manner of interaction. The counsellor works from the central hypothesis that the elucidation of the family's interactive process will create a context, a counselling system, in which the family's inherent capacity to change is stimulated. From this hypothesis the counsellor wishes, by inquiry, to reveal and unravel the family's interactive processes. The counsellor's practical aim is therefore to question in a way that releases new information to the awareness of family members. From this awareness there develops an understanding and from that 'doing something that makes a difference' then becomes a possibility.

Questions

Questions are therefore asked in a way that sets family members thinking, both individually and collectively about the implications of their answers. The questions are not designed to reveal 'facts' but to create a chain of reflexive thought in which the interconnectedness of the family as a system becomes apparent to its members. It is as a result of this 'new' thinking that ideas, feelings, behaviours and interactions come under the spotlight in a way that their change is possible. The mechanism of change therefore is focused on reflexivity rather than insight *per se* and it is reflexive in the sense that the answer of a person refers back to that person's activity in the system. This process is best illustrated by a statement from a woman giving feedback to an evaluative research project following a series of family counselling sessions; she and her husband had some problems in caring for their child with severe learning disabilities.

> and the counsellor asked me 'How do you choose the time you want your husband to help you?' . . . and of course I said 'but I don't choose . . . he just doesn't help.' Then the more I thought about it the more I thought perhaps I do choose, perhaps I do something different at different times. Then I thought 'I want him to help whenever it is necessary and I shouldn't "choose" and indeed he shouldn't have a choice about it.' Then I became a bit different, more forceful, assertive . . . in a nice way and things did change.

The 'answer' in the counselling session appears straightforward and almost factual but the questions stick in the woman's mind and reverberate within her way of considering the situation such that the belief emerges that she has a choice. Change then does result, from her perceiving her behaviour towards her husband in a different way and then altering her contribution to the interactive flow.

It is not clear in this example whether the counsellor intended this result by deliberately constructing the question to suggest to the client the notion of 'choice' within a system, or whether it was just something that happened. The point is that the effect of the question is determined by the client, not by the counsellor. The intentions and actions of the counsellor serve only to trigger a response; they do not determine it. Because of the nature of systems and the counsellor's part in the counselling system, she has no ability or even right to influence the family in particular directions. It is not possible to influence someone in a particular way. The counsellor can only be influential with her presence in the counselling system that is created. The counsellor cannot seek to take the process in particular directions but she can help construct a system that develops its own self-healing powers. As Hora (1983) points out, it is the clarity of understanding that has the power to heal not the counsellor, understanding being generated by the reflexive process. To illustrate this further, here is another example from the same evaluative research project. This time a mother is reporting on her experiences of family counselling for some behavioural problems with her 9-year-old daughter.

> The thing that sticks in my mind came at the end of a session and I think the counsellor was just joking. We were about to leave and she [the counsellor] said to my daughter, 'Tell me, were you born a pain in the neck or do you have to practise a lot?' and my daughter said 'Oh I have to practise a lot.' I had simply never seen my perfect little girl,

despite all the problems, as being a 'pain in the neck' and the fact that she seemed to be deciding to do it! Then I thought, 'Right madam, just like any other 9-year-old pain in the neck I'm going to deal with you.'

Clearly the counsellor could not have intended this outcome with perhaps what was a throw-away comment. The outcome was determined solely by the mother. The fact that the mother was only an observer of this interaction also demonstrates another advantage of questioning in a family, namely that when a number of family members are present they are all observers. Being an 'observer' of interaction about one's own family does give one a considerable amount of information. The responses of other family members are seen and heard and this in itself has an impact. However, the important aspect of this is that each family member will contrast their own answer to every question with the answer provided by other family members; they are thus confronted with the difference between their private response and the public response of the other person. Indeed the reflexivity of the family system can be defined as occurring within the continual recognition of differences between private thoughts and public statements and through this process of awareness, change can occur. In the last example above, the mother may have thought, 'silly question, can't answer that' but the daughter's clear reply of 'I have to practise a lot to be a pain in the neck' is in direct contrast to the mother's anticipated reply; it is doing something about the awareness of this difference that ultimately leads to interactive change.

Interventive interviewing

As the process of change can be set in motion by events that have not been directly intended by the counsellor, this has led to the development of what Tomm (1985) has termed 'interventive inter-viewing'. This is a perspective in which the range of opportunities for change is extended by considering everything a counsellor or therapist does during an interview to be an intervention. The counsellor is faced and indeed wishes to be faced with a situation in which she will never completely understand everything that is happening in a family but by utilizing natural fascination about the system's operation and by questioning the system, its operation becomes clearer to those who are members. In order to support her natural curiosity, the counsellor utilizes her awareness of the interconnection of the systemic life of a family as well as her knowledge of the tasks, trials and tribulations of the family life cycle. The counsellor has a view of the family as a system moving through time dealing with the evanescence of life and living. From this base the counsellor can frame a questioning stance, the stance of a very inquisitive observer of families. Questions are framed by the feedback received from previous questions and are given direction by the counsellor's inquisitiveness. Certainly such helping questions carry assumptions that can be politely termed prejudices (Brandon, 1983), but the questions are not designed to structure the answers but rather to encourage helpful listening, letting the speaker know that he or she is being focused on solely. Questioning and listening which does not structure the answer except minimally is a great art, and the counsellor offers her attempt at this art as an opportunity to the family to aid them in observing and listening to themselves, hence seeking ways out of the impasses they encounter.

Containing the questioning stance
The stance of questioning the system can only be contained within the traditional skills of counselling which come under the title non-judgemental active listening (Egan, 1990). The family counsellor will need to be able to demonstrate empathy and acceptance in order to facilitate this process.

Empathy
Empathy is essential for engaging individuals in honest and full participation in family counselling. The counsellor's empathic response encourages family members to express long-felt but incompletely understood and seldom voiced aspects of their experience. Empathy is therefore a tool for understanding, it being achieved by reflection of feeling and open-receptive listening. Once family members feel understood and accepted by the presence of a receptive listener, they acquire a sense of security and strength which allows them to declare their own desires and to be receptive enough to what others in the family want (Nichols, 1987). Empathy and non-possessive warmth are traditionally demonstrated by **reflection of feeling** (Rogers, 1967). This is a skill whereby the listener communicates his or her understanding of the other's felt experience. When this is done badly it becomes parrot-like repetition of what the other has said; well done, it affirms the individual's experience and at the same time intensifies the aware-ness of it, thus a feeling of authenticity is experienced. Rogers sees reflection of feeling as also a means by which the counsellor can check out her perceptions of the client's position. It is, therefore, a process by which the client's internal frame of reference is clarified within the context of a relationship. As 'feelings are the key to meanings', the experienced counsellor utilizing this skill can clarify

not only the meanings of which the client is aware but even those just below the level of awareness.

Empathy involves oscillation between thinking and feeling. It requires a deliberate shift from thinking and feeling *with* the individual (that is, a focus on the 'I'), to thinking and feeling *about* the individual (that is, a focus on 'me–you') (Schafer, 1959). The systemic counsellor resting on the element of empathy which is dyadic ('me–you') goes on to encourage the individual to consider the 'me–us' dimension by ensuring that other family members are given a 'voice'. By linking the experience of several family members the 'us' dimension of interaction emerges. This is achieved by the reflection of interaction in which the counsellor reflects back a short sequence of interaction that has occurred or has been reported on by family members. The systemic nature of human activity and experience is therefore revealed by the development of awareness and understanding that one's own thoughts, feelings and behaviour have immediate repercussions on the thoughts, feelings and behaviours of the other with whom we are in relationship. As with other things, it is not the counsellor's understanding that counts, it is the understanding that family members develop for one another. The counsellor in providing empathic understanding to all family members offers a bridge to improved communication, a transitional step in the development of possibilities for inter-action previously unavailable or unutilized in the family.

Nichols (1987) has argued that the use of empathy in family sessions is the means by which the 'elusive' self is brought out; it being elusive in the sense that it is hidden from view in the family system as it involves that person's meaning of their own activity within the family. The elusive self is indeed the beginnings of an appreciation by a person of their own systemic nature.

'Acceptance' – non-attachment

In offering empathic responses the fact that more than one person is present in the room presents a problem of a different order compared with individual counselling. In her discussion of systemic empathy, Wilkinson (1992) notes the need for the counsellor to also be aware of process. Not only does the counsellor need to demonstrate acceptance of each individual's thoughts and feelings but she also needs to demonstrate the same acceptance of the family as a whole. This is not straightforward for it has to be remembered that person A may have some negative thoughts and feelings about person B who is also present. Consequently every family member is watchful of the counsellor's acceptance of his or herself, of the acceptance of other individuals and of the acceptance of the family as a whole. Yet 'acceptance' does not truly convey the essence of this process because it implies a role relationship between an acceptor and the accepted. The counsellor is there to understand whatever reveals itself from moment to moment and is available to comment on it by her curiosity – by her questions. The counsellor has a point of view to direct her questioning, but the feedback from the family should constantly be changing that point of view. The counsellor is therefore present with receptivity to what is occurring; she is available to the family but in some way is also unobtrusive (Hora, 1983). Family members can be extremely sensitive to the counsellor's personal position on every issue, and each word and action by her will be scrutinized to see if it reveals 'taking sides' or blaming. Should the family perceive the counsellor being in any way judgemental, their response and orientation to change will be distorted. The family counsellor is therefore faced with the task of using her basic counselling skills to demonstrate acceptance, availability, unobtrusive receptivity and non-attachment to a number of people at the same time. As the counsellor has adopted a basic questioning stance, the framing of a question, the tone of its delivery and the response to the answers will be the means by which the family can appreciate the counsellor's acceptance of what is said and felt by everyone in the room.

In order to maintain a non-judgemental distance from the family interaction, the family should experience the counsellor in a 'neutral' role. Given the strength of blaming and guilt mechanisms in families, it is important that this neutrality is maintained throughout. Indeed such is the centrality of this neutral role that some theorists of family change have used the term 'Neutrality' to label their notion of acceptance (Palazzoli et al., 1980a). When used in this way neutrality refers to the position and role in which one is non-judgemental about the family process, it does not refer to an emotional non-involvement, it refers to a non-attachment to the processes and outcomes. As Cecchin (1987) has pointed out, this type of neutrality is best achieved by the counsellor having a permanent state of curiosity in her mind. By being wide ranging in her thoughts about the family, the counsellor entertains a multitude of possible descriptions of one interaction, hence one description does not become the 'truth'. The counsellor is not seeking the 'best' description or the most 'suitable' description from the 'most able' family member etc. The counsellor is interested in how all these 'descriptions' fit together in this family and what description might be useful for change now and in the future. The more inquiring a counsellor is, the more the family have an opportunity to reflect on their interaction through the realization that the counsellor can and does accept any formulation or description as she does not have any commitment to a 'right' or 'wrong' way of doing things. Different families will experience the neutral position differently and the counsellor needs to be mindful of this, especially where the counsellor and clients are from different ethnic groups. This is because different cultural contexts predispose the family and counsellor to respond to each other in certain ways, hence altering the nature of the inquiring relationship (see McGoldrick et al., 1982). The counsellor also needs to maintain the family's curiosity about herself, for if she does not then she is not producing any different information for them.

Basic skills

The tasks of conveying empathy and non-judgemental involvement are best accomplished through the practical skills of reflection of feeling and reflection of interaction. Reflection of interaction is important in that it permits the counsellor and family to move between individual frames of reference and the interactions those perspectives give rise to. These skills have been loosely described in this fashion by Raskin and Van der Veen's (1970) introduction to client-centred family therapy. By using these skills the counsellor will be able to show her caring for the family while at the same time exhibiting a distance from their interactive processes. The reflection process allows the counsellor not only to convey her understanding but also, as Campbell et al. (1989) note, to step back and observe where the family is taking her and reflect that back to the family in the form of a question.

The 'skill' of reflection therefore refers not just to the 'mirroring back' but also to the process of 'thinking about' in the sense of considering a wider meaning. Each individual therefore hears a reflection of his or her own statements, reflections of the statements of others, reflections of the family's interactions and wider reflections provided by the counsellor's questions. For her part the counsellor is feeding back what she sees and hears as well as offering her own perspective informed as it is by the family's thoughts, feelings and behaviour.

Putting together the differing basic practical elements of the change process, it becomes possible to construct typical short sequences of interactions that are found within the counselling session. It would be erroneous to consider that the interaction 'begins' in any particular place, but the simplest way is to start with the counsellor's question. Doing this we can construct two sequences, (a) the reflection of feeling sequence and (b) the reflection of interaction sequence. Each is shown in terms of a basic structure and a clinical example.

The 'reflection of feeling' sequence

Basic structure

Counsellor: Asks question of A.
A: Answers.
Counsellor: Reflects feeling from A.
　　　　　　Asks B about A's answer.
B: Answers.
Counsellor: Reflects feeling from B.
　　　　　　Asks B about A's answer etc.

Example

Counsellor: Mrs A, when your daughter argues with her father what is it like for you?
Mrs A: Oh it's so difficult. It upsets me so, I end up crying.
Counsellor: You become tearful?
Mrs A: Yes I just feel helpless, miserable really that I can't do anything to stop it.
Counsellor: So you feel inadequate and sad that you can't prevent it?
Mrs A: Yeah, that's about it.
Counsellor: I was wondering Brenda, you're in the argument so how does what your Mum says make you feel?
Brenda: Oh I know it makes Mum sad but I can't help that, the argument just takes over.
Counsellor: So you get to feel overwhelmed by the angry feelings so that you can't attend to other things?
Brenda: Yes, mmm.
Counsellor: Do you think you're good at attending at other times; are you good at recognizing when your Mum is sad at other times?
　　　　　　etc., etc.

Reflection of interaction sequence

Basic structure

Counsellor: Asks a question of A.
A: Answers.
Counsellor: Reflects interaction from A's reply.
　　　　　　Asks a question of B.
B: Answers.
Counsellor: Reflects interaction from B's reply.
　　　　　　Reflects interaction from A and B's replies.
　　　　　　Questions continue.

Example

> *Counsellor*: Mrs A, when your daughter argues with her father what do you do?
>
> *Mrs A*: I try and stop them.
>
> *Counsellor*: How do you do that?
>
> *Mrs A*: I say 'please stop' and then I tell Brenda to leave it lie, to let things be.
>
> *Counsellor*: So you want them to stop, you ask them both first but then you concentrate on getting Brenda to give it up ?
>
> *Mrs A*: Yes, that's right.
>
> *Counsellor*: Is that how you see things Brenda? Is that what happens for you?
>
> *Brenda*: Well I think Dad starts it, you know getting on at me and then I get on to him. Mum then tells us to stop arguing. You know she actually tries to get in between us but she always blames me, tells me it's my fault.
>
> *Counsellor*: Let's see if I've got this right. The argument starts. Brenda thinks her father starts it. I'm guessing you're not there Mrs A but you hear it. You come to where they are shouting at each other. Mum then stands between Brenda and Dad but then says a number of things, mainly to Brenda. Mrs A you see yourself just telling her to stop and Brenda, you see yourself being told off. [*Mrs A and Brenda both nod.*] So Mrs A what do you think when Brenda says you tell her off?

In both these examples, the counsellor is maintaining a position which does not imply side-taking or blame. She is attempting to be a very interested but detached observer who wants to get it 'right' not just for her own edification but primarily for the family's sake. She validates each individual by the empathy she shows and she validates the family as a whole by the way in which she switches from one individual to another and points out the way things are connected. These examples clearly focus on one or other sequence, but in session they are intertwined, with reflection of feeling and interaction occurring at the same time. Following this path the meaning of phenomena to the family will emerge, for meaning cannot be figured out, it only reveals itself through interaction (Hora, 1983).

The therapeutic encounter

In the family counselling system Napier and Whitaker (1978) note therapeutic encounters occur on three dimensions.

1 Initially the most charged encounter takes place between family members. The counsellor has the task of catalysing the opening-up process that allows for the creation of new

information and hence different interaction between family members. As the family come to trust the counsellor's ability to contain the difficult emotions and thoughts that arise, the intensity of the family confrontation deepens thereby allowing change to occur.

2   The second area of encounter is between each family member and the counsellor. In demonstrating her compassion, empathy and integrity she provides a model for relating that acts as a visible alternative to the family. This encounter develops in different ways with different individuals depending on their attitude, their personality, their age, their gender and their family roles, and this leads to the family appreciating the variety of modes of relationship that are possible within the composition of their family. These encounters lead to the development of a 'culture of caring' within the family necessary for it to go on and function effectively.

3   The final area of encounter is perhaps the most crucial and is built upon the increasing personal involvement of each family member and the counsellor herself in the counselling process. This is when each person encounters him or herself within that particular social context. Unless we each meet ourselves and are willing to meet ourselves, change, development and growth does not occur. This equally applies to the counsellor as it does to family members. Unless the counsellor intuitively and reflexively considers 'How am I doing? What sense am I making of this? What does this say about me?' then the family members cannot be expected to consider the same questions. As the process continues the 'open ground' looms ahead as the members of the counselling system create their own unique intimacy allowing each individual to experience their own authenticity. The separation between observer and observed disappears and a direct experience of a unity between helper and helped occurs. The power of healing is seen to reside within the process of the clarity of understanding and the creation of open ground no matter how momentary.

Linking the skills

Within the process of change that has been outlined everything the counsellor does is considered an intervention, therefore meeting the family, obtaining a description of the problem and understanding the meaning of the problem are all interventive. As the effects of any questions are determined by the client alone, ostensibly there is no difference between a question designed to elicit general descriptive information at the beginning of a meeting and a question put in order to encourage reflexive thought at its end. Therefore, although in the following chapters a distinction is being made between the skills of initially understanding a family problem and the skills that can produce change, in many respects they are no different. In the initial meeting the counsellor is more likely to follow her 'formula' for obtaining information and then in subsequent sessions allow the development of her hypotheses in response to the family's meaning to dictate the direction of sessions. But because the counsellor sees herself as moving from a more structured interview to one that feels more free-ranging, the family does not necessarily have the same experience of the interview process. Change in family counselling does not follow our formulations for planning sessions and it can often be haphazard. Therefore the skills required in the initial family session (Chapters 4 and 5) will find their use in later sessions, and the 'later' skills (Chapters 6 and 7) will be put to much use in the initial phase.

4

Meeting the Family

Our stern alarums chang'd to merry meetings,
Our dreadful marches to delightful measures.

William Shakespeare

When a family experiences a difficulty and help is provided, a number of other people become involved, a new system is constructed. Thus a grandmother has a hip replacement, her family are obviously involved in her care, as are her family doctor, her surgeon, her physiotherapist and the neighbour who helps out with the shopping etc. These other individuals collaborate with the family system to compose the caring system; these individuals are available in the environment that surrounds the family and are therefore part of its ecosystem. Each of the individuals concerned will be contributing to the woman's progress. But supposing no progress is made, and the woman does not resume her mobility in the expected manner, a member of the caring system may then make a referral to a professional who undertakes family counselling: 'Please see this woman and her family. She and they carry on in a way that keeps her dependent on others.'

The family meets the counsellor and immediately a counselling system is constructed. It is important to realize that this system did not create the problem, the problem created this system. Even though other professionals may consider themselves to be mere observers, the influence of these professionals has to be included. Similarly, the counsellor will need to recognize his contribution to the new system. The counsellor will need to be congruent in the Rogerian sense of recognizing his own involvement in the process. The family is therefore never immune from its connections to other individuals and systems and neither is the counselling system. When a counsellor is involved with a family it is impossible for him to treat its members as a group or a condition. He is already a part of them and is making a contribution which is not objective. However, this is not the view the family has.

In some counselling situations, the client arrives with the clear request 'I have a problem. I think counselling may help me with it'. This unfortunately is not the case in family counselling. Typically, family members and usually not all family members, present themselves as individuals who are concerned about one of their number. They believe this person has a particular difficulty which they, the family members, hope would benefit from some outside help. In this example, they may believe 'If Mother tried harder we wouldn't have a problem'. Families do not automatically have an encompassing interactive family life cycle perspective and indeed the gaining of this view by family members will be a primary goal of the counselling process.

The initial meeting – expectations and responsibilities

Families arrive for counselling with some preconceived notions and set expectations about what the problem is about and how it may be tackled. Because of this, in dealing with the initial meeting particular emotional themes need to be recognized and dealt with adequately so that counselling can commence effectively. These central emotions concern the issues of 'blame' and 'responsibility'. The most natural reaction to a problem that will not go away is that it must be somebody's fault. 'If only she tried harder with her physio and did something about it we wouldn't have this trouble.' Problems all too readily come to be seen as residing within someone, though that does not mean necessarily that the problem comes to be seen as residing within the 'identified patient' or that everyone agrees where the problem lies. For example, in the situation where an elderly parent is being cared for by a married son, the elderly person may be seen as causing a particular difficulty but the married couple may argue about the extent the problem was originally produced by the son's insisting on having his parent live in the family home. The adage seems to be that for every problem there is someone who is going to be blamed. This process of blaming in families is very strong and often influences the view the family has of professionals who may become involved with them.

There are those families who will look on the professional as taking responsibility for the problem. The undisclosed request being 'What are you going to do about it?'. A too sudden presentation of the fact that it is indeed the family's problem will undoubtedly give rise to the thought that the counsellor is blaming the family for the problem. Similarly, in other families the nature of the conflict may be such that a family member will feel that the counsellor is siding with a view held by particular members in the family and by implication is 'blaming' those individuals who do not subscribe to that view. The counselling task in this period of the process is therefore to create an environment in which 'blame' is irrelevant and responsibility is shared in an appropriate manner. This is best achieved by the adoption of an approach which clearly places the forthcoming work within the natural continuity of the work that has gone on before, both by the family and other professionals. The counsellor therefore provides messages to the family which do not imply that a new frame will be immediately placed on the proceeding. Meeting with a different professional, or the adoption of a different tack by an already involved professional, will be new enough information for the family to contend with.

Not only does the counsellor need to be mindful of actions which do not imply blame, but he will need to do this in a way that pays due regard to the expectations the family members have of contact with the counsellor.

Family expectations intially set the context for what occurs in counselling and tend to fall into particular types. There are those families who want the counsellor to talk directly to the 'person with the problem', the belief being that through this one-to-one process there will be some change in the individual and then all will be right at home. The second type of expectations tend to be about the belief that 'something, somewhere' will make a difference to the identified person and that the counsellor is the person who could arrange for the 'something, somewhere' to take place. Some expectations are then based on the view that the counsellor will offer an opinion, some advice or suggestions about the problem, with some families having a clear preconceived idea about what that opinion, advice or suggestion may be.

These expectations all focus on the counsellor being the person who introduces activity into the system. Such expectations are naturally in contradiction to the 'counselling' view, which would ultimately argue that it is the involvement of the family in its own activity that will make the difference to the finding of a solution to the problem. From the outset therefore there is a potential conflict of agendas between family and counsellor as the counsellor introduces the notion that activity will be shared by all and the ultimate responsibilty resides with the family. This conflict can be prevented from becoming a problem by the counsellor carefully dealing with setting up the initial meeting and the initial meeting itself.

Routes into counselling

There are two possible routes by which a family can arrive in a family counselling situation. The first route involves a referral by one professional to another professional; in a number of cases the referring professional may clearly specify that family counselling is required but depending on the professional context it may be the person who receives the referral who recognizes that the situation is one in which a family approach is indicated. In the second route the professional himself will have met with a part of the family system for some other professional task, a task which on assessment appears best dealt with within a family counselling framework. In these circumstances the professional becomes family counsellor for a definite period of time in order to meet particular goals which are defined within his general professional role.

In the situation where a referral has been received the counsellor will need to communicate to the family so that a meeting can be arranged. Obviously there is a variety of means by which this can be done but thought needs to be given to the nature of the message that the family are given in this communication. Some practitioners arrange to visit the family at home to brief them about the process that will occur when they are formally seen. This is done in order to encourage attenders who might otherwise not come. Pimpernell and Treacher (1990), for example, provide a learning experience about family work for clients through the means of an instructional video tape. Obviously not all workers go to such elaborate lengths to prepare future clients for the work at hand. A usual practice, however, is to write a letter to all the family clearly stating that it is helpful to meet all family members on the first visit and therefore if everybody could attend, it would prove beneficial (see Burnham, 1986).

Such views on preparation are based on the notion that an assessment of what has gone on before has been made, a decision has been reached about the outcome of that and activity of a different quality and direction will be pursued with the family. In other words, the view is that a service of a different nature is about to be provided to the family. It is, however, precisely the conception that something different will happen that necessitates the doing of something different. If one adopts a view that family work should be a natural continuation of what has gone on before, then there is no need for special pre-counselling activities. Continuity is the important message to provide, for the interactive perspective views current work as a simple progression of the way the problem has been considered and approached in the past. It is a continuation of the story. The message to the family is that it would be helpful if those involved could try to sort out the difficulties by using a few more ideas.

The most appropriate letter of invitation to attend is shown in the example below. In many senses this is a very straightforward appointment letter except for the fact that it needs to be personally sent by the professional and not just typed out by a computer. People do have a different response if they know they are to meet an individual rather than encounter some bureaucratic system.

> *Dear Mr & Mrs Andrews and Mrs Andrews Snr*
>
> *Your GP, Dr Jones, has asked me to meet with you to discuss the problems you are encountering with the care for Mrs Andrews Snr. I would be pleased to see you all at 2.00 pm on 23rd March at my office. Please let me know if this is inconvenient.*

This letter contains all the necessary information, both direct and indirect. Directly it provides place, time and ways to contact the professional concerned. Indirectly it is addressed to all the adults concerned and therefore provides some statement of who is involved. By placing Mr and Mrs Andrews first it structurally and politely acknowledges the centrality of this couple to the family. Next it clearly identifies the person who made the referral and his request that family members be seen. The problem is then mentioned by reference to a general problem identified by the referer, and, as the family will be used to that being identified as linked to a certain person, that person is clearly mentioned. The letter also carries with it the invitation for 'all' to attend and obviously the family will interpret that in their own way relevant to how they see the problem. In this example one of several things can happen:

1   The family put Mrs Andrews Snr in a taxi and let her get on with it.
2   Mr Andrews can arrive with his mother.
3   Mrs Andrews can arrive with her mother-in-law.
4   Mr and Mrs Andrews come together without the mother.
5   All three arrive together.

Whatever scenario occurs, it should be appreciated that whoever attends it is the family's response to that particular situation. It is their solution to the attendance problem and they will obviously take the action that makes the most sense to them and expresses their way of dealing with this particular set of circumstances. It will be the family's first statement of its position and perspective and as such it needs to be acknowledged and accepted by the counsellor. In each eventuality the family counsellor will be using his skills of acceptance and change promotion to aid the family move to an effective solution to their difficulty. Regardless of whoever attends, family counselling is defined by its perspective and skills not by the number of people sitting in the room.

Acquiring the attendance of important family members is well illustrated by the example of the route to counselling involving a professional deciding to meet some current professional goal within a family counselling approach, a typical scenario being for a professional to be meeting with just one family member when an issue is raised that indicates the most beneficial approach would involve more family members in the process of change. The family member, usually a woman, may have a variety of reasons for introducing the issue to that professional at that time and those reasons generally have nothing to do with the provision of family counselling services. In these circumstances the professional has to delineate clearly between the information he wishes to acquire in order to decide that a family approach would be helpful, and information that the family member is providing to promote her own perspective. Similarly, responding to this information needs to be done in a way that does not suggest the taking of sides or blaming somebody for the situation. As with all elements of the counselling process, a curious, quizzical stance regarding the family situation is one that will pay dividends. With this in mind, the aim is for the professional to give the family member the clear impression that he knows how to deal with these circumstances and to provide a clear statement as to why a family session would be beneficial (see Example 4A).

Example 4A

Mr and Mrs Appleby had a 5-year-old boy, a pregnancy some four months earlier had unfortunately ended with a stillbirth. The bereavement services offered by the Maternity Unit visited the home on three occasions and had only seen Mrs Appleby; they ceased their contact when she reported that she was getting on with things. The Health Visitor, who knew of this situation, visited routinely. During the conversation Mrs Appleby reported that the boy was waking at nights and coming into the parents bed and Mrs Appleby believed this was his upset over the death. The Health

Visitor asked about Mr Appleby's response to the situation and it emerged the parents were not able to talk about the issue because of the 'upset' about it. The Health Visitor felt that given the history it would be important to convene a family session. The words she used were as follows: 'Mrs Appleby, I know you have been trying to deal with this for some time but it seems to me that the situation is not improving. I think we need to consider the best way to help Darren deal with the death and help you and your husband be able to deal with that. The best way is for me to arrange to see both you and your husband to discuss what can be done about it. Now what would be the best time for your husband . . .

With this example the message is a clear one. 'It is understandable what is happening. It is best we use all the resources in the family to help matters. We can arrange such an occasion very easily.' Also, 'It is a natural part of my job that I do things in this way.' Such clear messages allow for the family to have a set of expectations for the session that immediately allows for the process of counselling to begin.

Box 4.1   Setting the initial meeting

The counsellor should:

1   Be wary of family blaming mechanisms.
2   Be careful not to appear to take sides.
3   Consider family expectations.
4   Present help as a continuation of what preceded.
5   Send clear straightforward appointment letters.
6   Make clear statements about organizing a meeting.

The initial meeting

At the initial meeting there are several clear tasks. The counsellor needs to say 'Hello' to everyone and introduce himself and the general professional task. He needs to set his understanding of the context of the meeting by being clear to the family about what is known. The family need to be able to offer their spontaneous description of the problem. From this the counsellor will be able to clarify the family's expectations of the meeting. Once this has been attained the task is to convey that the family's view of the problem and their expectations are understood. This then allows for the family and counsellor to redefine the task for themselves.

Saying 'Hello' to everyone and introducing self
[*The Andrews family were sent the appointment letter as above. They and a counsellor enter a room.*]

> *Counsellor:* Hello, I'm John Smith and I work here as a clinical psychologist. Are you Mrs Andrews?
> *Mrs Andrews:* Yes, that's right.
> *Counsellor:* Pleased to meet you. Do take a seat.
> *Mrs Andrews:* Anywhere?
> *Counsellor:* Yeah, that's fine. I guess you must be Mr Andrews?
> *Mr Andrews:* Yes. Pleased to meet you.
> *Counsellor:* Good, and you are . . .?
> *Mrs Andrews Snr:* I'm Mrs Mareeta Andrews.
> *Counsellor:* Does that mean you're Mr Andrews's Mum?
> *Mrs Andrews Snr:* Yes that's right. Pleased to meet you.
> *Counsellor:* Yes, hello. I hope these chairs are going to be comfortable enough for you.
> *Mrs Andrews Snr:* I think they'll be fine but they are a little low.
> *Mr Andrews:* We can help you get out when it's time to go.
> *Mrs Andrews Snr:* But it's not time to go yet is it?
> *Counsellor:* No, some time to go yet. Well it's nice to meet you all. As I said I work here as a psychologist and what I do is to meet with families to talk about their problems and worries. I guess this time it's just so you can tell me about whatever the difficulty seems to be and then we can see what needs to be done.

A relatively simple beginning. In analysing what takes place between people during this small period of interaction, how does this counsellor do? First we see that everyone is greeted personally and this would apply to children as well. In this case the first person that is greeted is the first person that enters the room. This person has the role of 'trailblazer' and in this sense acts as leader and protector for all those who follow. Where adults are concerned, it would be impolite and against the family structure to greet any other member of the family – it would be going against the family rules at this stage by insisting on greeting someone else first. In a situation where children are involved, matters are a little different for often families will push a child to the front to be the trailblazer in the manner of 'this is why we come – this is who we are presenting'. In these circumstances the first adult to enter the room should be greeted then the other adults and then the children. This approach maintains appropriate generational boundaries and gives the clear message that the adults will speak together first.

In the above scene the counsellor makes sure it is clear the exact way in which the individuals are related. In this case the mother/son relationship is so identified. This is necessary particularly when a number of adults enter the room. Not only is the counsellor to be clear about the particular familial relationships but he also needs to make these relationships publicly present as this provides the context for the counsellor to join the family. Politeness again dictates that identifying people as 'Mr and Mrs' is the means of acknowledging a marital relationship and there is no need to specify it in other ways.

The situation of meeting children can present particular difficulties especially in dealing with step-families. Too early a probe into the exact nature of parentage could provoke a threat for the family but there are ways of initially talking to children that allow for more information to come out. For example, it is possible first of all to ask the children who is the oldest, the next and so on and then have one of the children – the oldest or youngest – introduce the other children to the counsellor. Often doing the 'hellos' in this way allows the children to indicate who they are in relation to each other. Of course, as many step-families struggle with what to call each other, even in this very early stage of the counselling process the counsellor can give, in an interactive way, information to the family about how they can deal with each other. Some children are uncertain of using the term step-father/step-mother and many feel very awkward about finding a term to link this with their estranged parent – here they can be easily helped by saying, 'Oh so you started out with a different father. Right, I understand that and tell me what do you call this person here? People like me would call him a step-dad – do you know that word?' Such an approach is extremely effective for setting the scene of what is to come.

To return to the dialogue. The other thing the counsellor does is to make a simple comment about an everyday practical issue that is apparent to all the people in the room. In this case the counsellor is commenting on the difficulty an unsteady elderly person will have with the seating. Other comments may be on mundane matters such as the weather. 'Let's put your wet coats over here – it hasn't stopped raining for so long.' 'The children can sit and talk with us or they can use the drawing material – which do you think Mr and Mrs —?' 'I hope you found the building easily enough?' The messages in these comments are that it is permissible to talk about ordinary things. The counsellor is aware of everyday issues that everyone faces and therefore the counsellor is approachable. In the dialogue presented it can be

seen that this comment by the counsellor sets up a particular
family interaction. Mrs Andrews Snr links with the counsellor by
her 'seating' comment. Mr Andrews comes in with a statement
indicating that a problem, which has not been identified by anyone
except himself, can be dealt with but from the written word we
cannot ascertain whether Mrs Andrews Snr answers in a confused
or sarcastic manner. Whichever it is, one can easily appreciate how
this could readily develop into a interaction which is difficult and
distressful for the family. It is surprising how early on in the
contact with the counsellor families reveal their difficulties interactionally – but we are not ready for that yet. It is important that
the counsellor be able to demonstrate an ability to be in charge of
the process of the interview, particularly in the early stages. This
ability, known as structuring, has been supported in the research
literature as being positively linked with good outcomes (Gurman
and Kniskern, 1981) and such evidence continues to be found
(Green and Herget, 1991). Additionally, this skill linked to the
activity and direct guidance of the counsellor has been found to be
of particular importance in involving and maintaining men
positively in family work (Heubeck et al., 1986; Bennun, 1989).
Structuring of the session by the counsellor is therefore necessary
right from the outset as it clearly sets the context where
counselling and therapeutic work can occur.

In this dialogue we see the counsellor taking over this particular
interaction by making a matter-of-fact comment and then
immediately changing the topic on to an issue that is more
pertinent to the business at hand and undoubtedly not so explosive
for the family. In fact the counsellor goes on to outline the general
way in which he conceives of the task, which places some emphasis
on the talking about matters. He also suggests that the counselling
system, namely the family plus the counsellor, will undertake some
activity about the problem.

Box 4.2   Saying 'Hello'

The counsellor should:

1   Greet everyone and introduce self.
2   Discover familial relationships if not clear.
3   Be sociable.
4   Take charge of proceedings in a gentle way (that is,
    structure the session).

Being clear about what is known

> *Counsellor*:   OK. Well it is good to meet with you all. Right, I've had
> a letter from Dr Jones. He tells me that he has been treating Mrs
> Andrews Snr since she had her stroke three years ago and generally
> he is pleased with her progress. However he does think that
> sometimes you Mrs Andrews [Snr], could do a bit more for yourself.
> He says that he has spoken to Mrs Andrews about this because
> caring for your mother-in-law has not been without its difficulties.
> He is wondering how you all are dealing with the situation,
> particularly to ensure that Mrs Andrews Snr reaches her potential in
> every area. I sent you an appointment and then Mrs Andrews you
> rang me to ask if it was better if you all came or just you and Mr
> Andrews. I said that perhaps we could do more work if you all came
> but I left it up to your judgement about who could come. So that's
> what I know and have done. So, how can I help?

Essentially the counsellor has read out the referral letter with some
editing so that all the phrases or statements which ascribe blame or
negative motivations are changed or toned down. This is done to
present to the family the facts that are available as well as the
potential hypotheses that might be available, and to do this in as
neutral a way as possible. The aim is to present the facts as known
but not judgements about the facts.

The counsellor also provides everyone present with a brief
account of the contacts he has had with the family. Again this is
done to ensure that everyone is aware of what the counsellor
knows and in that sense, 'where he is coming from' is very clear.
This is only part of the message, for the counsellor is trying not to
come from 'anywhere' but is attempting to have the family realize
that he does not fully understand the situation and that his
struggle to understand what is happening is also their struggle. In
this sense the counsellor will, by his questioning, allow for a fuller
account of the problem to emerge; an account that is constructed
jointly by the family and the counsellor. The 'this is what I know'
statement clears the ground and allows the family to appreciate in
fact that the counsellor 'knows' very little, that his contact with
Mrs Andrews was minimal and therefore he is not likely to be
aligned with any particular person or idea. This also serves to
instruct the family that the counsellor does not have secret
conversations with anyone and that all his conversations with
family members will be made public in some way. The only
context in which the counsellor will operate is a 'public' one
primarily defined by the natural boundaries of the family and
hence change will emerge from the family's combined interaction
with him alone.

Box 4.3   Being clear about what is known

The counsellor should:

1   Present the basic facts as communicated by other professionals.
2   Present the basic facts of previous contacts with family members.

Gaining the family's spontaneous description of the problem

The usual family response to 'How can I help?' is for the family spokesperson to provide an account of the difficulty, typically intermingled with some history. This account will probably have been rehearsed mentally and the other family members will have certainly heard elements of it, though not necessarily in the full manner in which it is given on this occasion. Everyone in the room knows this bit of the interview will happen. Everyone is prepared for it and everyone, including the counsellor, will have some anxieties about what exactly will be said and how. As everyone will have to some extent fantasized about what this part of the interview will be like and because for most family members it will follow a predictable pattern, the manner of the report of the problem will obey particular family rules. At this early stage it will not be possible to identify what these rules are but it needs to be noted that family rules are very present at this moment. Any attempt on the part of the counsellor to ignore the presence of these rules and launch into an overstructuring of the interview will mitigate against a cooperative collaboration. The counsellor needs to listen, just clarifying essential details as they arise but essentially being a recipient of the information. How one elaborates on the story as provided will be discussed in the next chapter, but in this early stage of meeting the family, the important thing is to allow the story to be told as planned.

There are two potential scenarios to consider in this situation. The first concerns the situation where only the spokesperson speaks and the second is where there are interruptions, additions and alternatives provided by other family members. In the first situation, during and after the spokesperson has completed their account, some straightforward paraphrasing and summarizing skills are necessary from the counsellor but the essential element in the summary should be the implication, 'This is how I understand it at this moment' with the 'but of course things could change' very much in parenthesis. Other family members should then be asked whether or not they have anything to add to this beginning story, and for the sake of simplicity in this account of the counselling process we shall assume they do not have anything to add. In the second scenario where there are interruptions and the like, here again the need for the counsellor to demonstrate clear helpful structuring skills comes to the fore. It may be important to make statements such as 'Please, one at a time. I'll give everybody a chance.' 'I think it would be helpful if we let mother finish and then we'll check out everybody else's view.' 'OK, so your husband says it happens this way but you think it happens in a different way.' In this last statement we see one of the defining skills of an interactive approach, namely the ability to paraphrase and summarize on statements made by two people. The counsellor needs to remember who the spokesperson was and who, when and how the interruptions were made as this may be significant later.

As the family report on their problem, there is one particular area which may not be automatically covered by them and this involves the process by which the family found themselves with the counsellor. In order to understand how counselling fits in with the family's history and conception of the problem, it is important to have a view of the referral process. Some straightforward questions are all that are required in this regard. In the case that has been developing in this chapter, that of the Andrews, those questions might have been 'Who spoke to Dr Jones first about this – did you raise the issue or did he?' 'What did you think when your wife/daughter-in-law told you what Dr Jones said?' 'What did you initially think when it was suggested you come along to see me?' Such questions serve to place the family's natural description of the problem with their natural account of the referral process. This is done so as to develop the sense of continuity between the family's experience of the problem, their attempts at remediation, their contact with other professionals and the counselling process.

Another area that is not automatically reported concerns the attempts the family have made to correct the problems themselves. Again some straightforward questions will serve to elicit the information, 'When you realized there was a problem, what did you try to do with it?' 'Have you tried anything else?' 'What happened when you did these things?' Families respond very easily to these questions as they do demonstrate a clear interest in how the family themselves have tried to do something about the difficulty.

At the completion of this phase of the session, the counsellor should be able, in a summarizing fashion, to give a good account to the family of the problem as they see it, what they have attempted to do about it and how they find themselves in the counselling situation.

Box 4.4   Gaining the family's spontaneous description of the problem

The counsellor should:

1   Accept description as given.
2   Allow one account and ask other members for their additions.
3   If differences are present, paraphrase and summarize statements from two individuals.
4   Establish continuity with previous work by asking about the referral process.
5   Summarize information gained.

Being clear about the family's expectations from meeting the counsellor

Individuals and families do not come to counselling with a clear worked out view of what will happen. Few people have the expectation, 'I thought that we would talk about things and slowly I would have a different feeling about the problem and then constructively build some alternative strategies for dealing with it.' All of us when we have troubles, worries and distress do not think that clearly. But individuals will have imagined what will happen during counselling ever since the appointment was made. There may be several elements to these fantasies. First there may be 'magical thinking' that somehow the counsellor will raise the magic wand and everything will suddenly become different. Though most people are able to realize that thoughts of this nature are unrealistic, it pays dividends early on in counselling to recognize and reflect this feeling. Other elements of clients' fantasies will be related to those emotions underlying the initial interview, that is, 'blame' and 'responsibility'. Different family members will have different views about the counsellor blaming someone or taking some responsibility for sorting out the problem. Not only will these thoughts and feelings be present but family members may have specific expectations as to how the counsellor may behave which may or may not be realistic for professional behaviour in general and which may or may not be realistic for the counsellor specifically. Street et al. (1991) have briefly reviewed the theoretical issues and the process by which families develop a preconceived notion of the helping professional, notions which should be brought into open discussion in order that the professional may negotiate about expected and realistic outcomes. Crane et al. (1986) demonstrated that a therapist's ability to present the work as consistent and congruent with expectations is important to family members and a good prediction of outcome. For the family counsellor the important element in asking the question, 'What were you expecting to happen today when you saw me?' is the beginning of the negotiation process between the family and the professional about the tasks of counselling. This then automatically leads to discussion about change within the family itself. In response to these questions there are particular family responses which are identified below.

1   **Reluctant customers** – 'We only came because we were sent'.
2   **Action expecters** – 'We thought you would be doing something about this'.
3   **Opinion seekers** – 'We want your opinion on what's wrong'.
4   **Advice seekers** – 'We want you to tell us what to do'.
5   **Theory seekers** – 'We would like to understand why'.
6   **Counselling clients** – 'We thought that by talking about it we might sort something out'.

In each case the counsellor will be attempting to be as clear as possible about what the family expect. Some families will need help in differentiating between what they state they want and what they believe the counsellor is able to provide. As always, families will also differ in the extent to which they agree or otherwise with the spokesperson's verbal statements.

With those clients who are reluctant customers the counsellor needs to discuss with the family whether the counselling process up to the present moment has altered their perception in any way. 'Now that you've met me and we've started to talk about it, do you have a different view of coming along?' Some clients in this category are able to see that what is on offer will benefit them, but some maintain their reluctance. With this latter group the counsellor should discuss with the family the difference of opinion that exists, with the referrer thinking it would be a good idea for them to attend but them believing that they will achieve no benefit. In these circumstances the question would be 'Can you help me understand how the person who referred you thought it would be a good idea but you don't agree with that?' An example of this is provided in the following example.

Example 4B

Mr Aziz had a slow degenerative condition of the bones in his spine. He was unable to work. He reported frequent headaches which were not a typical or related feature of the condition. He also reported to his hospital doctor that he and his wife were not getting on very well and that his two teenage daughters were not helpful. His doctor considered him depressed and referred him for family counselling 'as there are clear family difficulties which are undermining him in dealing with his disability'. He and his wife attended a session with a family counsellor and both reported that they had only attended to please the doctor who had been helpful to them in the past. They both agreed that Mr Aziz's headaches had nothing at all to do with the family difficulties and they both believed these difficulties would resolve in time. Mr Aziz also felt that his headaches had not been investigated fully and that he really wished his doctor would undertake some further physical procedures. In fact it transpired that Mr Aziz was fearful that there might be a more serious underlying element to his condition and he had not been able to discuss this with his doctor. He was of the firm opinion that he would not require any further help until the cause of his headaches had been clarified medically. The counsellor asked the couple some 'what if' questions, particularly 'What if the doctor says nothing further physically was found' and both husband and wife were of the opinion that it would be 'a bridge they would have to cross' when the time came. The counsellor agreed with the couple that there was little point in offering any further appointments and he told them he would write back to the referring doctor informing him of Mr Aziz's views and indicating that he would be willing to see them in the future if they wished it.

As we can see from this example, the counsellor has used the session to identify the problem that exists between the referrer and the family. He has done this in a way that sharply focuses on the problem that needs to be addressed *from the clients' perspective*. In these circumstances the counsellor is asking himself the question 'whose problem was referred – the referrer's or the family's'. The counsellor is not attempting to enter into a discussion, debate or negotiation process with the referrer about this type of client. He is merely informing the referrer of the nature of the problem from the client's perspective. Here the counsellor is very clearly placing a boundary around the counselling context and seeking to engage clients who see the value of this boundary. It is not the counsellor's task to negotiate with clients to get them into counselling. He will naturally be using his skills to extend and focus the desires that clients arrive with and in some cases clients may indeed begin reluctant and then move as the session continues. Once it is clear that clients, as a family, are maintaining their position of reluctance then the problem is one for the referrer, not the counsellor. Such a situation usually implies that a professional has encountered some problem with a client believing it will be resolved via family counselling. Counselling then becomes defined by the problem within the professional task rather than the desires of the clients. Education with these professionals about how they themselves may utilize a family systems perspective, and how family counselling can fit into their overall management strategy, can prove very useful.

We should note here, however, that this discussion concerns only family counselling, for there are some varieties of family work in which 'reluctant' clients are seen. These clients would include those families referred via the judicial or statutory system for work following juvenile crime, child abuse, substance abuse etc. These types of families require a particular set of skills to help overcome their reluctance and these skills are not within the ambit of family counselling. For work of this nature, the reader is referred to Dimmock and Dungworth (1983), Crowther et al. (1990), and Weakland and Jordan (1992).

The next type of category of client are the action expecters. These are families who clearly expect the counsellor to take some action from his own professional position, such that it will make a difference to the family problem. The most typical action being hoped for is that the counsellor will persuade some institution to do something different as this will resolve the difficulty the family have, the usual institutions being schools and education authorities (for children's problems), housing departments (for all sorts of problems), or residential homes (for elderly people). In these circumstances the counsellor will, in this initial stage of meeting the family, attempt to help them clarify the exact nature of the problem and their exact expectations of what will happen should the institution take the action they require. Once this has been done the counsellor then needs to spend some time on the question, 'What would happen if the institution refuses to do as you suggest?'. Some families may move their position after reviewing their own answers to this question as well as their experience of the initial interview and they may indeed become clients. Other families may maintain their action-expecting position and in this situation skills to work with institutional as well as family systems may become necessary (see Conyne and O'Neil, 1992).

Each family of action expecters will in some way set a dilemma for workers whose professional practice is not solely within the field of family counselling. These families will pose for the professional questions about 'Should I stick to the family counselling model here or use my other expertise? Where is the dividing line between my role as a counsellor and my role as a professional with another task?' Obviously the experienced professional will be able to use some counselling skills as and when necessary within general clinical practice. However, all professionals need to be absolutely clear about those occasions on which they are resting on the change mechanisms of counselling and those occasions when they are not. This is especially important, for in counselling most families there is a period of 'feeling stuck' for both counsellor and family and this period needs to be travelled through. For this reason family counsellors do require ongoing supervision which will be discussed in Chapter 8. An example posed by this type of client is presented in the next example.

Example 4C

Mark Amery, aged 10 years, had developed a stammer which was first noticed by his class teacher and he was referred to a speech therapist. The usual methods of helping a child stammerer did not appear to be effective in this case. The speech and language therapist, who had only seen the mother, considered that the reports of his father's rather rigid authoritarian approach and his mother's over-concern for him were important aspects of the problem. She therefore referred them on to a colleague who specialized in a family counselling approach to these types of difficulties. When the family attended the family session it became apparent that the parents expected the counsellor to arrange with the school for Mark to change classes. They believed that this would stop Mark's problem. The initial family session went well but the parents insisted that no further progress would be made until Mark changed classes. In answer to the question, 'What would happen if he changes classes and the stammer stays', Mr and Mrs Amery were clear that the family would return for some family sessions. The counsellor decided that her role in these circumstances should not involve negotiations with the school and she informed the family that the original therapist could request that the school consider a change of class and therefore the counsellor would write to the therapist suggesting this. The letters were sent and Mr and Mrs Amery eventually discussed the matter with the school who took the position that because of resources it was better for Mark to remain in his current class. Mr and Mrs Amery accepted this and immediately contacted the counsellor to arrange for them to be seen.

In this example it may well have been the father's involvement in the initial counselling session that made the difference to the outcome, but whatever the reason for this, the action of the counsellor in being clear about the boundaries of the counselling situation were important in that they orientated the family towards future possibilities via counselling.

Those clients that come to the family counselling situation seeking opinions, advice and theories are the type of families that can very readily be helped via the counselling interview process to become counselling clients. In dealing with these families the counsellor has to judge how firmly the family hold on to their view of the counsellor in the role of opinion provider or advice giver or theory explainer. For many families the only way in which they can conceive of formally seeking professional help is to ask for opinion, advice or theories and then, when they encounter the self-reflexive process of the interview contained within the counsellor's warmth and acceptance, they readily enter into the process offered. Other families, however, hold on to the view that the end of the counselling process will be when the counsellor finally makes some pronouncement and in doing so the matter then becomes concluded. There are particular ways in which the counsellor can construct a view, frame opinion or create a theory using the family's own view and experience of the problem and these methods will be outlined in Chapters 6 and 7. The important point at this stage in the procedure is that the counsellor is clear about what the family expect of the counsellor and how they expect the counsellor to meet these expectations.

Box 4.5 To be clear about family expectations

The counsellor should:

1 Ask what the family are expecting of the counsellor.
2 Demonstrate acceptance of responses.
3 Negotiate the boundaries of counselling from the replies.

Giving feedback on the family's view of the problem and their expectations of counselling

During this phase the counsellor will be saying a good number of times, 'Now have I got this right' and then feeding back as neutrally as possible the story as the family have recounted it together with their expectations. The counsellor, however, will be making some changes to the actual account and, as with all summarization, it will not be a simple verbatim report. The counsellor will feed back the story in terms of its historical development so that the family acquire more of a sense of their own process through time. Providing feedback in this way is helpful in that it begins the process of the family distinguishing between those events that occurred serendipitously, those events due to the actions of others and those due to the actions of themselves. It also allows for a 'logic' to develop so that the family appreciate the actions they took themselves to remedy the problems and what further action, including work with the counsellor, may be involved. To return to the Andrews family whom we met earlier, the counsellor has now moved to giving this feedback.

> *Counsellor:* Now let me see if I've got things right. Up until two years ago, Mrs Andrews Snr, you had been living alone and were well able to look after yourself. You had done this for five years since the death of your husband. Out of the blue you suffered a stroke and were in hospital for about six weeks. You've had physiotherapy initially for some time and that got you moving around again. After the stroke it was clear you couldn't live as easily at home and the family had to make some decision about this. The alternatives were to live with your daughter or your younger son, Mr Andrews here. Mrs Andrews you were the person

who had to get people together to make a decision and when that happened it was agreed your mother-in-law would live with your family which includes yourselves and your two teenagers. You all knew it would be difficult but you felt it was for the best. Now since that time Mrs Andrews Snr, you've been struggling with your disabilities and you do find it hard sometimes. Mr Andrews you're not certain whether your mother could try harder but regardless of this, you think the doctors have not been clear about how much change to expect for her. Mrs Andrews you feel your mother-in-law could make more effort with her own care – sometimes this has caused difficulties for you all and occasionally you've had words about it.

Mrs Andrews you were consulting your family doctor about some problems that you think may be the first signs of the menopause and you mentioned to him the concerns you have about your mother-in-law and the difficulties this has caused you. Dr Jones felt there were some issues to discuss and so he told you that he was asking me to see you and he mentioned this to Mrs Andrews Snr. It sounds as if what you are hoping for is that I will give you some advice, though I'm not sure if that is about how Mrs Andrews Snr could be helped more or how to help you all agree about things.

In providing this summary it can be seen that the counsellor has included issues in a particular way that lays out the matter in a family life cycle manner. The older woman has dealt with the loss of her partner, is now dealing with her own failing health and the issues of dependency/independency provoked by this. The married couple are dealing with the potential change of their roles as their children deal with their own independence while at the same time dealing with the dependency of an elderly relative. The children, who have not been met yet, should be preparing to set out on their own autonomous life's course. So, in life cycle terms, this family's struggle is clearly related to the theme of dependency and how the family, as a unit and as individuals, are dealing with this and this will constitute the principle background theme.

The counsellor has also identified other individuals who may have a significant role to play, and in particular we have Mrs Andrews Snr's daughter and the two adolescents who live in the household.

As yet we cannot be certain of the importance of Mr and Mrs Andrews's particular life cycle issues, especially whether Mrs Andrews was waiting until the children had almost left before embarking on some individual career path or whether she had made that decision some time ago. There are also many other issues left unclarified – the relationship between the family and Mr Andrews's sister; the exact nature of the things Mrs Andrews Snr

will not do for herself; the issues about which Mr and Mrs
Andrews 'have words'; the way the children are affected by the
issues etc. In providing this summary 'story', the counsellor not
only has indicated his ability to listen and convey to the family his
willingness to begin to see the problem from their 'agreed'
perspective. He has also pointed to issues that at this time remain
unclear and confusing but which can be discussed later. In some
senses the counsellor has made his understanding of the problem
the central task of this phase of counselling, for in the elaboration
of his understanding the family themselves should find a new
meaning for their own difficulties which could aid a reappraisal of
the problem. To add to this process the counsellor has taken the
story the family has presented and clearly given the message that
the recounting of this description is the beginning of the process of
counselling.

Box 4.6   Giving feedback on problems and expectations

The counsellor should:

1   Summarize all elements of the family's description.
2   Relay the description as a historically based story.
3   Mention those individuals who may have a role.
4   State those areas of uncertainty and lack of clarity.

Defining the basic counselling task for family and
counsellor

The provision of feedback marks the phase in the initial meeting
when the family's primary mental rehearsal comes to an end.
They have arrived, met the counsellor, told their story. He has
heard it in a way that is recognizable, he is aware what they want
and so . . . The family are now at a stage where they will be
entering unexplored territory in which their guide is the counsellor,
but it must be borne in mind that the counsellor does not have a
map. The counsellor's skill is in helping people learn to draw and
read their own map. It is at this stage that the counsellor can set
out in plain terms what needs to be done to embark on a process
that may ultimately involve change. The counsellor at this moment
is defining a task that can be met by the family and himself
combined. It is making a statement of how the 'counselling system'

will begin to operate and go about its business. The Andrews family again –

> *Counsellor*: Well it seems to me that as a family and as individuals you struggled with some difficult things over the years and for some reason the way you deal with problems is not helping you as much as it can do. I'm not sure that I understand all the things that have happened and in particular how certain things got decided. I'm not even sure I have a clear idea of what the exact problem is. What I would like to suggest is that I try to make some sense of what is happening and this obviously is not as simple or straightforward as it sounds because you each will have different views on what is happening. I also don't know whether your daughter, Mrs Andrews Snr, should come along at some point and the children may have something to say at some stage. What I'm saying is I'm not sure but I think it would be helpful if you help me understand. So perhaps we could begin by Mr Andrews, you telling me . . .

The message here is clear: 'I don't know. Help me find out.' The counsellor also refers to some topics that could be discussed and who might be involved at a later stage. It should be noted that in this statement the counsellor makes a clear number of 'I' statements. He is making it very apparent that as a person he is involved and has a view which is relevant to the situation. (Obviously the view he has which is most helpful at this stage is 'I don't know'.) The importance of doing this is to allow family members to appreciate the professional as a concerned individual who allows a personal contact within his professional role. Such a statement of personal involvement gives permission for the family similarly to be personally involved as it removes elements of the formality of the professional/client situation. Again for those counsellors who come from an individually based tradition within counselling, it should be recognized that such personal contact can occur relatively swiftly in the family context simply because the presence of family members removes some of the minor rules of social convention that operate in the one-to-one situation.

The personalized and 'unknowing' way the task statement is made means that there is no requirement to enter into a discussion about what is to happen. The counsellor does not know and does not understand some things and the way matters are to proceed is for everybody to ensure that ultimately he does understand. The 'unknowing' counsellor is therefore acquiring some freedom to act within the family system because 'not knowing' cannot and does not conflict with anybody's view and it certainly removes the initial threat that somebody will be blamed. Making the statement in this way does mean that the unravelling, reconstructing process can begin immediately and so the counsellor in the above example moves straight into the next phase of the interviewing process. The majority of families accept this very readily for the way the counsellor set up the initial part of the session will have, in some way, prepared them for what is essentially the continuation of the family's story. Some family members however will have particular concerns and anxieties that will emerge at this point, not so much in terms of disagreement about the overall task but more to do with the statement of their position within the family and the 'protection' they may feel that position requires. Within the example we are dealing with the following interjections from family members that occurred.

> *Mrs Andrews Snr*: Oh I don't think Jennifer my daughter, could come. She is very busy you know.
> *Counsellor*: Yes, different people are busy in different ways. I'm not sure yet if we need to ask her but if it looks as if her coming along might help us all, we can discuss the best way of arranging it then.
> *Mrs Andrews*: Will you be talking to our doctor about the best way to get Mum out of the house sometimes?
> *Counsellor*: I'm not sure yet about what you really need advice about. I'm not sure. I'm not ruling out making some suggestion to you but at the moment I'm not sure on the best way to do things.
> *Mr Andrews*: Will you be telling us the best way to stop having these terrible rows about the situation?
> *Counsellor*: Well, it does seem as though the ending of the rows would be a good indication that things are getting better for you. As yet I really don't know enough to even begin to offer some advice. Once the situation becomes a little clearer then the solution may naturally suggest itself – but we'll have to wait and see about that.

The counsellor deals with these statements, requests and demands about the task in a matter-of-fact way. As the statements are clear enough, the counsellor feels no requirement to reflect back what is said. He responds directly. In each case his response indicates that all things are possible if they appear to be right for everyone. At the moment things are still in a state of 'unknowing' and he cannot say whether or not they are right. These statements from the counsellor serve to orientate individual family members to the overall task, it lets each know that each can and will be heard but that no sides will be taken and no ready-made solution will suffice. The manner of the counsellor's responses also prevents him from falling into the conflictual traps present in all families and they model to the family how by adopting a certain orientation, potential conflict within the family can be avoided constructively.

Box 4.7   Defining the task for family and counsellor

The counsellor should:

1   Paraphrase the family's struggle.
2   Refer to issues and persons that could be involved.
3   Make 'I' statements.
4   Adopt a 'not knowing' stance.
5   Deal with requests and queries in terms of future possibilities.

The counsellor has now met the family and has set the basic counselling task. The next phase of the counselling process, considering the current problem, is dealt with in the following chapter.

5

Considering the Current Problem

We are what we think,
All that we are arises with our thoughts,
With our thoughts we make the world.

Sakyamuni Buddha

Introduction

Having met the family and orientated them to the interview task
the counsellor will now move towards that section of the interview
which focuses more intensively on the difficulty that has brought
the family to counselling. There are two dimensions to consider in
achieving an expanded view of the current problem:

1 The meaning dimension.
2 The interactive dimension, which involves two elements:
   (a) Tracking interaction around the problem behaviour;
   (b) Observing the interactions in the counselling room.

The meaning dimension

In order to deal with the amount of information that bombards us
in our social relationships, we each develop ways of categorizing
information and linking these categories together so that in some
way they organize and predict how our world will work. The
psychologist George Kelly (Kelly, 1955) has described humans as
scientists when he outlined the way in which we use our own
categories, or constructs as he termed them, to build a 'theory' of
how the social world is happening for us. Kelly's work, however, is
not solely focused on individual processes for he formulated
interpersonal and social action elements to the way individuals
construct their world (Dallos, 1991). He particularly stressed that
people are psychologically similar not by virtue of similar experience or behaviour but rather because they use similar constructs in
similar ways. For example, those adults who construe poor table

manners in children as 'bad' and 'disrespectful' are similar in that they have shared constructs. This obviously has an importance for how families conduct their business. Kelly also suggests that for any two people to interact effectively, they need not necessarily share the same constructs but they should have some constructs about how the other sees the world. So not only do we have a 'theory' about the world from our perspective but in order to relate to another, we have a 'theory' about the perspective of the other.

The similarity of two individuals' constructs and the view those individuals have of the other's constructions obviously interrelate in a manner that produces interactions of a varying nature:

1 If both individuals have similar 'shared' constructs and are reasonably accurate in viewing how the other sees a particular situation, then the individuals will tend to act in unison about · that situation.

2 If the individuals have different constructs and are reasonably accurate in viewing how the other sees the situation, they will be able openly to express their differences and the basis for beginning to negotiate joint action will be present.

3 If the individuals have different constructs and are inaccurate in viewing how the other construes the situation, they will be in conflict, which may or may not be overtly expressed and the basis for negotiation of a solution of joint action is problematic.

4 If the individuals have similar 'shared' constructs and are inaccurate in viewing how the other construes the situation, then conflict will be present, again overt and covert, and the individuals would need to appreciate the nature of their shared constructs in order for a solution of joint action to be found.

Obviously these generalized possibilities have a considerable bearing on the counselling task.

It can be seen that the constructs that individuals have, be they shared or otherwise, embody the notion of how action and behaviour from the past and present are viewed as well as providing information about what action is necessary for the future. To return to the bad table manners example, if somebody construes this behaviour in a negative way then it does suggest certain things that can be done, such as telling children off, not inviting certain children to your home etc. The meaning that is ascribed to any situation therefore carries information and it serves to 'regulate' what is to be done in the future.

Within some families therefore each member will be constructing his or her own set of meanings for any behavioural event. This set of meanings will then dictate how the past is viewed, how the present is dealt with and how the future is planned. Some meanings will be shared and others will only be held by individuals. It is this that constitutes the family ideology.

The counsellor therefore has the task of assisting the family in communicating about the meaning they ascribe to their problems. He will be looking to identify those areas where they have a shared view and those in which they are in conflict. As the meanings are revealed, the basis for moving towards negotiations for solutions becomes a possibility. Andersen (1987), Cecchin (1988) and Epston and White (1989) have all developed ways in which a counsellor, in meeting with a family, may gain access to their view of the world and be of assistance to them.

In order to develop the practical tasks of inquiring into the family's meanings, we will use the example of the Charles family. John Charles, a 10-year-old boy with cerebral palsy, was referred by his school to an educational psychologist because 'he may be school phobic'. He, his mother, father and 15-year-old brother, Martin, attended the initial interview. In their presentation of the problem Mr and Mrs Charles tended to talk across each other and the counsellor needed to use his structuring skills to ensure that each took their turn. At the end of the initial phase of the interview, the counsellor established that John was not cooperative in going to school and Mrs Charles had described how she felt that her son was 'distancing himself'. Mr Charles was more concerned about the activities of the school. Mr Charles was uncertain of his expectations about the family session but Mrs Charles felt that the counsellor would talk to John 'on his own'. The counsellor now needs to inquire about the meaning ascribed by family members to the problem behaviour.

> *Counsellor*: Mrs Charles, you've explained to me how John won't do as he is told and how he seems to be distancing himself from you. As you think about it, what sort of ideas and explanations do you have for this happening?
>
> *Mrs Charles*: Oh I don't know. [*Seems slightly tearful.*] Well, I think he doesn't like the fact that he is handicapped and he is getting his own back on me.
>
> *Counsellor*: Oh right – that's a hard one for you [*look at husband, who looks somewhat vacant*]. So do you have any ideas about changing things?
>
> *Mrs Charles*: I know it's difficult, you haven't got a magic wand or anything and heaven forbid we can't put the clock back, but if you could only help him and if he could accept it, things would be different, I'm sure they would.

Counsellor: Right, so is that where your expectation comes from, that I should spend some time with him?
Mrs Charles: Suppose so.
Counsellor: So how would you know if things were getting better – you know, what needs to happen so you know the problem's gone?
Mrs Charles: Well I don't expect him to be an angel. I guess he would talk to me more and tell me things.
Counsellor: So if you felt he wasn't so distant – right? . . . Mr Charles, what do you make of what your wife says?

In inquiring about the family ideology, the question to ask of each individual is 'How do you think this has come to happen?' It is important not to ask this as a 'Tell me why?' question in a bold, bland way – a mistake of many beginning family counselling. This question needs to be asked in terms of suggesting that you are inquiring about one person's view but other people can have a different view, i.e. alternatives could be available, none of which is fixed in stone. A good phrase for this question is, 'As you try to explain it to yourself, what sort of ideas do you come up with?' Such a question will clearly allow an individual to express his or her theory about the problem. Each family member can then elaborate on their perception of the reported problem as well as publicly stating their associated felt experiences. This will and then should be linked to the question of what needs to occur in order to eliminate the difficulty – after all, this is what theories are for. The counsellor is attempting to establish the currency for future discussions, i.e. those feelings and issues which are central and are important for creating the relationship with the family, and obviously the counsellor will have used reflection of feeling much more than has been presented in the written word here.

Meaning ascription
In the example above we see a theory that is unfortunately all too common in chronic illness and disability, namely that the person with the problem is doing something to express their great displeasure at being disabled and that they are trying to get their own back in some way. Naturally with any person who is suffering from a chronic condition there will be feelings of non-acceptance, frustration etc., and these may be manifest in a variety of ways, but the family counsellor can only deal with those feelings as they emerge in the session in the context of the family interaction.

Family members can have other inappropriate 'theories' about behaviour. For example, when an elderly person has a dementing condition the family may view memory problems as being motivated: 'She forgets deliberately, you know.' Inappropriate meaning ascription can readily overlay class, culture, ethnic and gender prejudice. 'He behaves like that because his father came from such-and-such country.' When faced with unhelpful meanings the seemingly correct professional action may seem to be to provide the family with 'the correct' information. At this stage of the counselling process, however, the counsellor needs to understand how this particular set of meanings is embedded in the family system and therefore the possible imparting of information is left until meanings and interaction have been clarified further (see Chapter 6). Too rapid a contradiction by the counsellor would undermine the potential for change. In the dialogue we see how the counsellor links Mrs Charles's theory to a particular future event, namely how she will know when there is no longer a problem. Her reply about John being close to her reveals another aspect of her theory, namely that closeness to her will prevent future problems. At one level, Mrs Charles's request to the counsellor is about helping her feel closer to the boy and this will need to be fed back to her in some way.

A central feature to note in meaning ascription is that invariably the person who is ascribing the meaning believes that someone else needs to do something in order for the situation to change. Therefore the future aspect of any meaning tends to be a focus on future actions by other family members rather than the meaning ascriber. If we take Mrs Charles for example, within her meaning ascription she believes that her son needs to behave differently so that he does not seem so distant from her and, as she believes he 'needs' help with this, she wishes the counsellor to take the necessary action to ensure this. Here the future actions of her son are linked to Mrs Charles's expectations of the counsellor. It is important that the counsellor be clear in helping each member specify what they perceive as being the necessary future action as this highlights areas of potential cooperation and conflict in the family as well as the likely pressures there will be on the counsellor to act in certain ways. Typically the counsellor is 'invited' to become involved with a particular family member or even an agency in order to 'solve' the family's problem. Street (1985) has described how such invitations lead to the counsellor being *triangulated* within the family, that is, the counsellor merely acting within the family's dynamic in a set way instead of allowing the dynamic between family members to express itself. What can unfortunately happen in this situation is that the counsellor ends up in a dyadic interaction which has been defined by another family member and this then undermines the aims of counselling and is hence counterproductive.

In this regard it is worth looking at a possible scenario from an inexperienced counsellor's session. Mrs Charles has told the counsellor that she feels her son is not accepting his disability and because of the mother's expectation that the counsellor should help her son, a particular type of interaction follows:

> *Counsellor*: John what do you feel about what your mother says about you and your disability?
> *John*: I'm not sure. I don't think about it very much.
> *Counsellor*: Well do you feel the same as other boys your age?
> *John*: Well I don't know. In most things its OK.
> *Counsellor*: In what way is it not OK? . . . etc.

Here we see the development of a dyadic interaction between counsellor and boy which has been defined by the mother, that is, it is all about 'the lad accepting his lot'. This is mother's meaning – and a meaning that comes from a family situation in which there may be conflicts about meaning. We have no way of establishing the truth or reality of anybody's view. All we can do is help family members move towards their solution of their problem and this is achieved much more by moving the question around the family: 'What do you think about what your mother/father/son/daughter/husband/wife has just said?' This question maintains the family focus and prevents the counsellor entering into unproductive interactions. Indeed a good tip for the beginning family counsellor is whenever you feel stuck in a family session and you are not sure how to proceed, it is worth while asking one family member about what another family member has just said – it keeps the session going very well and prevents the pressure towards triangulation.

In the example, the counsellor is dealing with the meaning the mother ascribes to the behaviour and the emotions associated with these meanings. The counsellor will use them as information to establish how the family interacts generally. In essence the counsellor deals with the here-and-now of the mother and then asks how father responds to this by asking the question, 'What do you think of that?'. In this situation, because of generational boundary issues, the counsellor will initially focus on the parents, returning to the children's view later. It is important to recognize that in asking family members about the views of other members the counsellor is attempting to construct a composite picture. He is not setting about to establish a 'truth'. Returning to the example:

> *Counsellor*: Mr Charles, what do you make of what your wife says?
> *Mr Charles*: I'm not sure. I think he is getting picked on in school and the school are labelling him as the problem when other children are more to blame.

The father seems to be virtually rejecting his wife's views and feelings, so we may query how supportive the couple are to each other. We have, however, established his theory which is different and hence potentially conflictual with his wife's.

There is one further element of meanings that can be investigated, which again aids in the construction of a general consideration of the problem. This involves the notion of 'catastrophic expectation' which has its origins in *Gestalt* therapy (Perls et al., 1973). This notion is that an element of our theory will be a view of the action we need to take in order to prevent the catastrophe we dread happening. Put in simple terms, the question to the client is 'What is the worse thing that could happen if this problem continued?' Let us look at Mr and Mrs Charles's replies.

> *Mrs Charles*: Oh John would be depressed and miserable and he would cut himself off.
> *Counsellor*: So I guess you feel you need to sort this out so you can help your son feel OK and so you don't lose your relationship with him. And what about you, Mr Charles?
> *Mr Charles*: If the school carry on the way they are going, they are going to make my boy a delinquent because once you label a child they will behave that way ... and I don't seem to be able to stop it.
> *Counsellor*: So for you, the actions of others are forcing John into a certain way of behaving and you feel powerless about this?

With these statements from the parents there should be ample opportunity to ask each to respond to the other, to explore the fears each has and what may be helpful in being supportive to each other. Occasionally, if some family members have theories which seem to focus on the counsellor taking on a responsibility, it may be worth while saying, 'I've guessed you thought about what I might say – what is the worst thing I could say to you?' Once again the purpose of eliciting the response to this question is to make available for discussion the fears seldomly openly expressed and discussed. On this occasion these fears will concern the activity of the counsellor himself and therefore it can serve as a good starting point for negotiating the appropriate client–counsellor relationship.

Now would be a good opportunity to make an inquiry of the boys. The generational boundaries have been respected by asking the parents; it has been established that different views do and therefore can exist; and the counsellor has already indicated that he views the mother's statements about him seeing John as a request that flows from her, the mother's, theory; the counsellor does not respond to it as a demand.

> *Counsellor*: · John, why do you think there is a problem going to
> school in the morning?
> *John*:   Don't know.
> *Counsellor*:   That's fine. What about you Martin? What do you think?
> *Martin*:   Well, it's just difficult.
> *Counsellor*:   Difficult?
> *Martin*:   Yeah [*Looks away*].

John and Martin are indicating they have little to offer the session
at this point. John might have said something like 'Don't like
getting up in the morning', in which case, in language appropriate
for a child, the counsellor could have explored his theory in the
same fashion as he did with his parents; and similarly with Martin.
The counsellor will, from time to time, need to check out if they
wish to make a contribution; the counsellor will determine this
depending on when he feels he needs to indicate that the boys can
have a 'voice' if they choose, while respecting the rights and
responsibilities of the parents as an executive subsystem.

In this discussion so far there has been a focus on the
conflictual, unhelpful element of meanings. To imply that this is
always the predominating element would be erroneous. Often as a
family elaborate on their meaning, some potentially shared
constructs emerge and hopeful solutions are suggested. These have
to be recognized and acknowledged but again the counsellor needs
to complete the sharing around of the family discussion before
moving towards that phase of the session when future solutions
could be suggested.

> *Mr Charles*:   I suppose I do feel powerless about the school, but when
> I say that, I'm then not sure whether they or we should do
> something.
> *Counsellor*:   How do you mean 'we'?
> *Mr Charles*:   Me and my wife, we might be getting it wrong in the
> way we're dealing with him.
> *Counsellor*:   Do you mean 'jointly'?
> *Mr Charles*:   Yes jointly. Perhaps we could be doing something
> together.
> *Counsellor*:   Well there may well be something you can do together but
> could we hold that for a moment, while I just go over this. As I'm
> understanding it, Mrs Charles, you seem to be focusing on how John
> is dealing with himself and perhaps yourself in this situation and, Mr
> Charles, your focus has been more on what the school could be
> doing but you don't sound so sure of that now. It would, however,
> help me if we could move on . . .

As always, the counsellor feeds back the information he has
received in a manner that does not approve or disapprove of any

statement or view but in a way that exhibits concern and interest for what is actually expressed between family members.

Box 5.1   Inquiring into meaning

The counsellor should:

1   Elicit each person's explanation for the problem.
2   Elicit each person's immediate view of other family members' meaning.
3   Assist each family member in stating their view of the necessary future action.
4   Ask the 'catastrophic expectation' question.

The interactive dimension

Tracking interactions around the problem behaviour
From the family's view the problem they are encountering is limited to a particular set of behaviours and interactions. The family systems view, however, considers that any reported problem is contained within a much wider interactive pattern than that necessarily considered by the family. The notion used to explain this is that of 'punctuation of interaction'. To any family each 'set' of interactions is separated from others with a beginning and an ending. Much as with writing a sentence, you start with a capital letter and end with a full stop and punctuating words in this way gives a particular meaning separate from other meanings around it. However, the systems view is that life is just a continual stream of interactions (the words) and that where one places the beginning and end (the capital letters or full stops) is arbitrary. Each means of punctuating interaction can make sense in its own right. The notion of punctuation implies that any observable behaviour is part of a larger pattern of interaction. The counsellor therefore has the task of exploring the interactive element of any reported problem and expanding the length of that interactive sequence so that the family can, in their own way, arrive at their own new punctuation. To do this they need to come to appreciate how the problem is embedded into how they interact generally.

Although the work to date with the family has had particular aims and foci, it does serve to prepare them for the exploration of the interactive dimension in which the counsellor constructs an interactive picture of what occurs around the primary reported problem.

The counsellor needs to select, with the family's help, one instance that would represent the reported difficulty and from that instance work back and then forward in time so that the full sequence of events can be appreciated. Nearly all the spontaneous reporting that is done by family members tends to be interactive shorthand: 'I tell him to get ready for school and he just doesn't.' The mother, perhaps her husband and John understand this way of describing matters but it just does not convey the information that is necessary to a curious observer. It is, metaphorically, a speeding up of time. The danger is that family members accept the speeded up version as what is happening, whereas a closely observed version will contain more choice points where a difference could potentially occur. A useful analogy is of a video tape of the family interaction; the family's version is composed of a fast-forward view omitting some of the beginning and some of the end. The counsellor needs to be able to construct a version for himself and the family which covers a longer period of time in slow motion and perhaps with some freeze-framing.

Counsellor: OK, I wonder if we could consider a specific incident of him not doing as he was told, Mrs Charles. Would yesterday be OK? – Yeah, OK. Let's imagine we had a video tape of what happened. What would I see?

Mrs Charles: Me shouting, come on, come on, get going.

Counsellor: When would this be?

Mrs Charles: Trying to get out of the house.

Counsellor: OK. There might be some other important things that happen. It would help me if we could go back a bit. Let's see, who gets up first?

Mr Charles: That's me.

Counsellor: What do you do – you know, about the kids and . . .

Mr Charles: I get up before everyone; get ready; have some cereal. I take my wife a cup of tea and I call the children.

Counsellor: How do you do that?

Mr Charles: Call the children? . . . I just pop my head around the door, tell them it's time.

Counsellor: And what do they do?

Mr Charles: Just grunt, I don't expect anything else [*laughs*], and then I leave.

Counsellor: So you basically see to yourself, you do tell the kids to get up, there's no real conversation or discussion [*father nods*], your wife gets a cup of tea and you're off?

Mr Charles: That's it.

Counsellor: OK. Do you hear Dad go in the mornings, John?

John: Yeah. [*Martin nods.*]

Counsellor: Right, so you are awake. What happens then? [*Turns to Mrs Charles.*]

Mrs Charles: Well I get up, get ready, lay out things for school and breakfast.

Counsellor: While you're doing those chores, do you say anything to the children?

Mrs Charles: Well I just might shout up the time, if I don't hear much movement, but then I check on John.

Counsellor: Sorry, do you always check on John?

Mrs Charles: Well now, yes, I always do about twenty past eight because he doesn't seem to have moved.

Counsellor: What happens?

Mrs Charles: He's supposed to get up himself. He's big enough and capable enough but when I go he's not moved at all.

Counsellor: So are you waiting for Mum, John. [*John shrugs his shoulders.*] Does he say anything to you or you to him, Mrs Charles?

Mrs Charles: Oh you know, he becomes what I call 'snivelly'. 'I don't want to Mam . . . must I . . . No don't want . . .'. Things like that. I end up having to dress him. [*Looks at John.*]

Counsellor: How are you with him? Do you shout, get angry, are you kind, you know how . . . how do you deal with him?

Mrs Charles: Well shouting never did anything. I just persuade him and I suppose end up doing most things myself. I suppose I pamper him a bit just to get things done.

Counsellor: Are you thinking or feeling anything about this?

Mrs Charles: No really. Just a bit fed up as you know. It's too much at ten years of age and I've got a lot to do, but it's better I get him going this way 'cos we'd never get anywhere if we left it up to him.

Counsellor: Let me see I've got this right about this bit. You get up, call Martin and he gets on with it. You go and check on John and he's just not done anything and it's not that he refuses or gets stroppy, he's sort of just reluctant [*looks to mother and she nods back*] and you end up doing things for him because that way you find things get done. Is that right?

Mrs Charles: Yeah, that's right. I know you're not supposed to give in to children but it's the only way I get anywhere.

Counsellor: Right, and you know how best to deal with kids and you don't like doing what you do but in your situation you get things done which is better for you.

Here the counsellor is slowly tracking through the interactive chain, being sure that each link is dealt with sufficiently so the development of the interaction over this particular time span is understood. Here too we see how Mrs Charles' initial description of the problem – 'I tell him to do something and he doesn't do as he is told' – conforms to some extent to what may happen but when placed in the overall context of the enlarged interactive description, we have constructed an image of a child being reluctant and whiney and a mother undertaking all of his tasks for him. Here then we can observe the process of opening out the problem in such a way that individuals and families can, by observing their own inter-actions, consider taking different types of action.

This piece of dialogue also demonstrates the skill of 'reflection of interaction'. The words used to describe each action are quite neutral and may in fact be the words the family themselves would use to describe that actual piece of behaviour. At this level the function of the reflection is to slow the interaction down in the minds of family members, giving them the opportunity to think about a series of events which they have grown used to. At another level the counsellor may introduce new words to describe what is happening, or perhaps even provide a label which has not been provided before. In the example, the counsellor, after establishing John as being awake, describes him as 'waiting' for his mother. He then takes Mrs Charles's description and identifies John's behaviour as being 'reluctant' rather than 'snivelly'. Of course, the use of such words has implications for how individuals will think, feel and act. In the example we can see that the reflection produces a response from Mrs Charles for she clearly feels ill at ease about 'giving in' to the child. The interaction with the counsellor has brought to public awareness that (a) she may know that another course of action could be recommended but (b) because of her own feelings, she does not take it. These thoughts and feelings of hers are then accurately reflected in the traditional way by the counsellor.

It can be seen from the example that questions about the details of interactions generate much more information than the description initially offered by the family. Although the family are not in any sense wishing to withhold information from the counsellor, they will need to be prompted to provide information. The counsellor must hold a flexible attitude about the potential way any interactive sequence can develop. In the above dialogue the counsellor takes the time-frame backwards from the 'going to school' moment to the moment the family get up. By this method a more comprehensive picture emerges.

As the interview progresses the counsellor will be tracking events at different points in time and events in different contexts. In the above example, the counsellor should ask about the continuation of the interactions of trying to get John to school, as this is the issue that was spontaneously reported. Similarly the counsellor would be well advised to ask about interactions around occasions where John behaves in a similar fashion; this too will provide useful information for everyone.

The family may also not spontaneously report on how the other.

family member fits into the interactive pattern they are reporting but the counsellor can ask about this. This inquiry question is inspired by the knowledge that if anyone is present at an interactive event it is impossible for them not to be part of that interactive event and not to communicate. The general principle of considering the action of others present needs to be applied constantly. In our example the counsellor turns to ask the brother, Martin, about his action.

> *Counsellor*: When Mum is trying to persuade John to go out through the door, what do you do?
> *Martin*: Oh I tell him not to be so stupid. That he's a pain. It gets on my nerves.
> *Counsellor*: Do you do that a lot, everyday, sometimes?
> *Martin*: I suppose I make snide remarks most days.
> *Counsellor*: Mm, Mm – and well, what happens when you make your remarks?
> *Martin*: Oh Mum shouts at me, tells me off that I'm interfering and hindering.
> *Counsellor*: Does she tell you off in the same or different ways to John?
> *Martin*: Oh she really shouts at me. She's kinder and 'Come on Johnny' with him.
> *Counsellor*: Right, so Mum's saying 'Come on please John' getting in the car and you're there watching and you'll say something like 'Don't be so silly,' and your mother shouts at you, really tells you off?

In this example we see how another possibility has developed, namely that Mrs Charles knows how to shout at the children and potentially she could shout at John. As John and Martin are able to take part in a verbal discussion their involvement is developed in a way that is appropriate for their age but even at this age children may appreciate the availability of drawing materials while they listen and talk. Children's contribution to family work is essential. Carpenter and Treacher (1989) identify three ways in which their involvement is useful

1 As signallers or 'co-therapists', by making direct verbal statements or clearly communicating something by their play.
2 As verbal participants, as we can see in this example.
3 To expand the focus of discussion by making available another set of relationships to act as a context for the themes and interactions being discussed.

A number of authors have specifically addressed the manner in which younger children can be approached in family sessions (Dare and Lindsey, 1979; O'Brien and Loudon, 1985; Dowling, 1993).

Many of the skills recommended by these authors are extensions of good communication skills with children that should be a natural element of effective parenting. The counsellor should therefore not only display an ability to communicate directly with children but to do so in a manner that does not undermine parental authority but enhances the parental knowledge of effective parent–child communication. Sokolov and Hutton (1988) provide a useful introduction to communicating with children in their work specifically aimed at parents.

Another means by which the counsellor expands the interactive context of the problem is to extend the time when the problem behaviour ends. In a commonsense way it would appear that the end of the sequence of events of trying to get John to school is when he actually walks through the school door and mother gives over responsibility for him to the teachers. This undoubtedly is the way the family punctuate the problem. This punctuation, however, neglects to take into account the interactive reverberations of the problem on other individuals and groups of family members at other times. In each and every case a problem experienced in one part of the family will to a greater or lesser extent have some effect in another part of the family. Part of that reverberation will be how the family discuss the problem. To inquire about this will give some information relevant to how problems are solved and feelings dealt with in the family. In this example the couple relationship is one in which one partner (mother) is more active in the problem sequence than the other, it therefore becomes especially necessary to clarify the interactions occurring when the mother reports on the problem to her partner. Here the counsellor's aim is to track the interacting about how problems that require solutions are reported, the manner of that reporting, the solutions considered and the emotions aroused by that, and finally how those emotions are dealt with.

> *Counsellor*:   Mr Charles, if your wife has a struggle with John in the morning, do you find out or know about it in any way?
>
> *Mr Charles*:   Oh I know when I come home just by the look, you know I can just tell by the way my wife is.
>
> *Counsellor*:   How would I know that look; how would I know what it means?
>
> *Mr Charles*:   Quite easy really. She wouldn't really look at you. She would be quiet and trying to keep a distance and her face would be very pained.
>
> *Counsellor*:   Oh right. When she's like that, what do you do?
>
> *Mr Charles*:   I'd say, what's the matter. She wouldn't answer for a while. I might ask again and then she'd tell me all about it, being irritated and upset.

Counsellor: What kind of things would she say?

Mr Charles: 'I've had a difficult time with John. He just wouldn't do things' – you know, things like that.

Counsellor: Sort of 'its been very hard for me' [*husband nods*] and what do you say?

Mr Charles: Oh not sure really, try and sort the problem out.

Mrs Charles: Well mainly you tell me how much you are worried about it and how unhappy you are with the school. [*Turning to the counsellor*] Sometimes I think I'm going to have to stop him going to the school and becoming angry with the Headmistress.

Counsellor: Oh let's see if I've got that. The way you, Mr Charles, find out about the problem is by looking at the way your wife is when you get home; you have to ask her about it. Mrs Charles, you tell him it was a difficult morning for you. Mr Charles, you say how worried you are and perhaps that you are angry with the school and Mrs Charles, you have to calm him down a bit because he is angry. So how does that end?

Mrs Charles: When he's calmed down I get him some tea and we carry on.

Counsellor: OK, so am I right, you don't manage to talk about possible alternative ways of dealing with things?

Mrs Charles: That's right. I suppose that's why we've come.

The counsellor has been able to link separate interactive sequences so that the family's response, particularly the executive subsystem's response to the problem, has been constructed. At this point in the interview the counsellor may consider it worth while offering a major summarization of the interactive sequences, including John and his mother, the brother's behaviour, and how mother and father talk about the matter at the end of the day. Such a summarization is the beginning of constructing a framework in which an unofficial 'contract' for future work is made as this outlines the family's problems to themselves in another way and hence indentifies the interactions the counsellor and the family are interested in. It additionally serves to 'teach' the family the process by which the counsellor will proceed.

The counsellor, however, is not just attending to the interactions that 'actually' happen. He is also interested in the interactions in this situation if some potential changes were made. The counsellor is therefore interested in tracking interactions around the problem with some seemingly minor differences of personnel and context. It is, for example, important to go through possible situations in which the main characters are changed. So, in this chapter's example, the counsellor would be interested to know what would happen if Mr Charles had the responsibility for getting the boy to school. Although we know that this is not practically possible given the requirements of his job, the questions would allow everybody to appreciate the potential of different outcomes following different actions by individuals.

> *Counsellor*: Mr Charles, let's suppose you were not in work for a while and your wife was visiting relatives. It would then be your responsibility to get John to school. What do you think would happen?
> *Mr Charles*: Well I perhaps would be more forceful than my wife . . . not give in so much.
> *Counsellor*: Would that be about the time he'd have to get up?
> *Mr Charles*: All the way through, just be more insistent.
> *Counsellor*: And what do you think John would do?
> *Mr Charles*: Well he'd just have to do it.
> *Counsellor*: So you think that you would get somewhere with him by being 'more insistent' I think you said?

Here we note that perhaps an underlying difference of parental strategy is present. It would be too early in an initial session to focus directly on the potential conflict between the mother and father and this issue simply becoming public is judged as being sufficient for the present moment. However, it would appear worth while to pursue an understanding of the interaction that may or could occur when the parents attempt to undertake a joint action.

A good question would be 'What would happen if you both tried to get John to get himself ready?'. The answers to this will yield several pieces of useful information such as the potential behaviour of the child in this situation, which would expand the understanding of his repertoire of behaviour. Also it could indicate the potential outcome if the couple join forces, thereby expanding the possibilities they might entertain as a solution to their difficulty. Perhaps more importantly it would reveal the usual interactive pattern when both become involved in a difficult situation.

> *Counsellor*: What would happen if you both tried to get John ready himself?
> *Mrs Charles*: Oh that won't work. My husband would shout at John, John would cry and probably I'd get upset and tell my husband off.
> *Counsellor*: Is that right Mr Charles [*he nods*] and how would that situation end?
> *Mrs Charles*: My husband would go off in a huff and I'd end up pacifying John.
> *Counsellor*: Oh I see, and does that happen often?
> *Mr Charles*: Yeah, it used to happen a lot but it wasn't getting us anywhere so I just decided it wasn't worth it and backed off.
> *Mrs Charles*: No it didn't help at all. At least now we've stopped arguing about it.

Not only now do we have an idea of how John, Mrs Charles and Mr Charles interact when matters are difficult but we have also gained some important historical information; the interaction we see now as being related to the problem is in fact the end result of a failed strategy for dealing with a similar problem some time ago. The counsellor would need to feed this information back to the family and bear it in mind later when problem solving strategies are sought.

Box 5.2   Tracking interactions

The counsellor should:

1   Select a representative interactive sequence to follow.
2   Carefully construct the interactive chain of events of the sequence.
3   Ensure that interactions are reported on events 'before' the problem and 'after' it.
4   Ask about the actual interactions of others seemingly not involved.
5   Ask about the potential interactions if the personnel change in the situation, particularly if two or more family members combine action.
6   Demonstrate reflection of interaction.

The interactions in the room
Families do not interact in a random fashion. Their interactions in particular contexts follow patterns that the family have set up over a period of time. These patterns will emerge as a result of all the factors involved in any set of circumstances. The counselling situation itself provides a task for the family to perform and their usual interactions in problem solving situations will come into force. In the room the family will interact in a manner that will have some bearing on the way they interact about the problem and tell us something of their general interactive style. It is quite probable that certain interactions observed in the room will be similar to interactions significant in maintaining the problem. Although certainly in the initial session, and perhaps even in the second session, it is early days to comment on the similarity between the interactions in the counselling room and the reported interactive patterns as they occur elsewhere. The counsellor needs

to be mindful of noting patterns, for at some stage these will be important to feed back to the family.

In our example family we can note particular themes, even through the limited information presented:

1   Mr and Mrs Charles have an interactive pattern whereby Mrs Charles plays the major role in confronting any problem, exampled by her dealing with John and becoming the main spokesperson once the session had been structured.
2   The older boy interferes with John's management but only to a limited extent and he has not interfered or interrupted in the session.
3   Mr and Mrs Charles have tried to act jointly but it did not seem to be effective.

There are other possible patterns but as yet these will be dealt with more adequately as hypotheses rather than patterns that are clear and recognizable. For example, Mr Charles's potentially being either angry or not being involved with John. The clarification and elaboration of other patterns and the testing out of some of the counsellor's hypotheses will need to be left to other sessions.

At this stage of counselling, it is only possible to consider that we have some evidence of those patterns that have been mentioned and the counsellor will need to commit these to memory to inform his thinking and questioning. Obviously following the session the counsellor can keep some notes as an *aide mémoire* but it is important also to develop the skill of memory – a memory for a set of interactions. This is the type of specific memory that comes with experience and is common in other skilful enterprises. For example, it is known that if you show a very experienced chess player a chess board with the pieces in mid-game, with only a little exposure the player would be able to reproduce it accurately. Such memory operates by the player having some means of committing to memory the set of relationships of the pieces on the board by bringing into operation a higher set of constructs and structures which are unknown to those of us inexperienced in the complexities of chess. Similarly with family interactions, the beginning counsellor tends to deal with each interactive sequence as a single entity and is not easily able to commit it to memory in a way that allows for it to become accessible for comparison with another set of interactions later. Counsellors develop their own set of constructs and structures about family interaction which allow them to retain more information and make it available for use later in the session.

In terms of those particular patterns in the Charles family, the least threatening one is the possible pattern that the children do not overly interfere with the problem behaviour or with the parents' management of it. So the counsellor will need to 'reflect' this in some way. 'From what you've said and what I've seen, it looks as if the other lad doesn't interfere so much in this problem – am I right about that?' The counsellor is here training the family that he will comment on the link between events inside and outside the room and this serves to make them more aware of the means by which they all interact.

Pulling together what is known

It is now possible to pull together all the information we have about the Charles family and it falls under three headings:

1 The life cycle issues.
2 The meaning the family have of the problem.
3 The interactive sequences and patterns around the problem.

The life cycle issues

We have a family who potentially could be entering a stage where the children's development means there is less need for active parenting and more potential for the parents to undertake their own interests. This immediately has a greater potential and a greater risk for Mrs Charles as it involves her in ceasing to be a full-time mother and perhaps pursuing some other activity. At this stage we do not know how Mr Charles would respond to such a change of role for his wife.

This normative stage of development could be threatened by the nature of John's disability. Can it be assumed that with his cerebral palsy he will be able to fall into a normative developmental pattern or will he require some different parental help. In this respect some thought will need to be given to the extent that he is potentially a typical 10-year-old and moving slowly towards the autonomy of early adolescence, or whether he and/or his disability is a hindering factor. Clearly how the family deal with this will be important and to a large extent will depend on a realistic appraisal of John's needs.

The meaning the family have of the problem

There is no overall agreed meaning of the problem even at a basic level between the parents. This indicates the presence of a conflict in the family ideology which is not being resolved and which does not help in finding a solution to the difficulty.

The older child thinks that John is being a 'baby' and this may be a reference to his reluctance to face normative developmental issues or perhaps it indicates some jealousy about the attention John receives.

Mr Charles has the view that the school is causing the problem and his fear is of John being labelled as a difficult child, this meaning resulting in his feeling of powerlessness.

Mrs Charles feels her son is becoming distant from her and perhaps this is a comment on usual developmental processes, as one would predict children moving towards autonomy may seem not so close to parents. Mrs Charles is clearly fearful that the problem indicates some ongoing difficulty with John's way of dealing with his handicap.

Interactive sequences and patterns

John is reluctant to get ready for school. Mrs Charles, although resenting it, takes over most of the actions which he could be responsible for.

Mrs Charles and Mr Charles do not listen to each other's feelings about the difficulty. They talk across each other and no problem solving behaviour occurs. They do not engage in any joint action about the problem and they seem to have an ineffective interactive sequence for dealing with their difficult emotions.

Moving on

We have seen how knowledge of the life cycle issues has led to some particular questions, but in the main the life cycle theme remains the 'hypothesis of the counsellor' as it has not been effectively shared with the family. The family meaning and interactive sequences have been fed back to the family and their reactions and responses explored. The counsellor has by now inducted the family into the counselling process, the family know the counsellor will ask questions, will track interactions, will be allowing everybody their turn appropriately and will be feeding back to them continually. Having done this the next task of the counselling process is to promote change through counselling skills, although formally this is another phase and will be dealt with here in other chapters, it is a task that merges naturally into the tasks outlined in this chapter. Family counselling is an activity that once the initial phase has been completed a flowing conversation takes place between family and counsellor, and even though matters are being dealt with in these chapters in a compartmentalized form, by this stage of the counselling process the flow is flowing. Let us move on.

6

Using Counselling Skills to Encourage Change

> In the beginner's mind there are many possibilties, but in the expert's mind there are few.
>
> Shunryu Suzuki

Having met the family and acquired some understanding of the current problem, the counsellor then needs to use a variety of skills and interventions to encourage the change process in the family. She will need to clarify many issues and open up communication; as this occurs some maladaptive patterns may emerge and these will need to be interrupted. The family may then need help to link the past, present and future. At some point it then becomes important to impart information. Throughout, the counsellor will need to support those adaptive changes that become apparent. The types of questions that cover these areas have been outlined by Tomm (1987, 1988) and the framework for specifying these counsellor's interventions is shown in Box 6. 1.

Box 6. 1   Counsellor interventions

Basic interventions	1	Clarifying and expanding.
	2	Opening communications.
Specific interventions	3	Breaking maladaptive patterns.
	4	Linking past, present and future.
	5	Imparting information.

Although these particular activities could easily be undertaken in the sequence indicated, it would be inappropriate to consider that this sequence is the one that should be followed. Each family and each problem will require differing degrees of emphasis and order. Therefore the list only serves as a possible menu for the counsellor to select from.

To illustrate how each of these categories of skills can be used, we shall introduce another family. Mrs Davies is a 50-year-old woman who has diabetes. Over the past six months she has found it difficult to maintain stability of her blood sugar level. Her physician considered that this was unusual and was related to stress. He asked the support worker to investigate primarily whether 'psychological factors are involved'. Mrs Davies attended the first session alone during which the focus was on recent family history and she reported feeling stressed and worried about her family. Her husband had been made redundant some nine months earlier and was reported as being somewhat miserable about this. The family had two children, a 21-year-old son who lived elsewhere in the town and a 15-year-old daughter living at home. It emerged that the son frequently came home to stay and he and his father often argued. Sometimes the son and daughter also argued. Mrs Davies agreed to bring other family members for a family session but at the appointment only the mother and children appeared. The counsellor at this stage had little idea of the major family interactions or their ideology. In terms of the life cycle she thought that the family were in the phase of the children leaving home and the parents were faced with the task of renegotiating their relationship. Unfortunately, Mr Davies's redundancy had interfered with this process.

Clarifying and expanding

Throughout any session the counsellor will be attempting for the family's benefit to clarify the process of any particular sequence of events and the meaning put on those events by participants.

Families become quite fixed in how they view a problem and the events surrounding it, a feature being that each individual will somehow assume that a friendly observer will see the events in exactly the same way as he or she does. Each will also assume that the words they use to describe the events will instantly convey an exact impression of what occurred. The counsellor's task is to very gently confront these assumptions by asking questions and in this process the family becomes aware of new elements in what was previously considered to be familiar. Clarifying the descriptions of individuals and expanding on the meaning that they ascribe to these descriptions is therefore a basic intervention that occurs throughout counselling. This is done initially by 'slowing down time', and then making a link to another level of meaning so that the individual and family begin to experience a degree of flexibility in their thinking.

In order to move between time frames it is useful to concentrate on the meaning attached to the interaction. Pearce and Cronen (1980) specified six levels of meaning which relate to each other in a circular fashion and which relate to the time classes of sequences of Breunlin and Schwartz (1986), described in Chapter 3. In each family it is possible to consider not only each level in turn but also the potential links between each level. Thus if we take the situation of the counsellor discussing with Mrs Davies why her husband has not come, in Mrs Davies's words the six levels of meaning could be:

1 **Content**:   He says he is not bothered.
2 **Speech act**:   He said he was not bothered but he was very angry about it.
3 **Episode of interaction**:   I took a long time to tell him about the appointment and I'm afraid I then blurted it out that he had to come. He got angry saying he wasn't bothered.
4 **Ongoing relationship**:   This is how it is, he spends a great deal of time telling me he's not bothered and I'm fed up with him just being like that.
5 **Life script/family myth**:   I don't know what it is but all the men in our family don't bother when it comes to something important.
6 **Cultural pattern**:   It just might be because he comes from that part of the country, you know where men just do what they have to and don't bother about family matters.

It is unlikely that any one individual would easily and rapidly travel through all six levels of meaning. It is far more probable that an individual will remain at just one level and the counsellor's task therefore comes to link that one level to others, thereby not only clarifying the nature of the particular meaning but also expanding that meaning considerably. In this particular example Mrs Davies's comments were mostly at the speech act level which is at the first class of time sequences. To assist the clarifying process the counsellor needs to ask a question that links two time frames:

Mrs Davies: He said he was not bothered but he was very angry about it.
Counsellor: Is that something that is typical in your relationship or is it only about this issue?
Mrs Davies: It is typical of those things which seem to be important to me, makes me feel fed up as if he's not bothered about me at all.
[*Later in the counselling*]
Mrs Davies: As I said, it's as if he is not bothered about me.

> *Counsellor*:   And is that similar or different to other marriages in your family?
>
> *Mrs Davies*:   Well I suppose you see it's a bit like my mother and father but she seemed to put up with it all and I try not to do that.

Another very effective means of clarifying and expanding is to ask questions of the family about the things that they actually observe. Once the family realize that the counsellor is attempting to frame a composite view of the events in their home then they readily come to answer questions from the observer's perspective. The observer's perspective insists on the person being involved in what is going on. Certainly before one can take new action in any particular social setting one needs to be able to 'observe' it. It is, for example, difficult to empathize with another person when one is unable to make some observations of the experiential condition of that person. It is often the case that each family member simply believes that everyone sees or should see the same situation as him or herself. Observer-perspective questions serve in helping family members become aware of the situation as it is seen by each person and in doing this each individual is given the opportunity of clarifying exactly what happens for everyone else. So each person can expand their vision of what is taking place. It is of course possible for the counsellor to make statements about what she sees as occurring, and although this may be useful at some points, statements only set forth positions and views. Questions therefore have the advantage of helping the family develop better observational skills which is useful when they reflect on their own behaviour or their contribution to some interactive pattern. Also, as family members develop a realistic view of the situation from their own experience, they are more likely to trust in their own capacity to find solutions to their own problems. Hopefully the end result of this is they feel that counselling simply served to unlock their latent talent for self-healing.

> *Counsellor*:   Andrew, your mother said she blurted out about your father having to come along. How did you see that?
>
> *Andrew*:   Well I don't think she blurted it out. Dad is so difficult to get close to, you have to shout very loud for him to notice. It was the only way for her to do it.
>
> *Counsellor*:   OK is that how you saw it, Sue?
>
> *Sue*:   Well I wasn't there. These things usually happen when I'm not there. But there are different ways of doing things with Dad.
>
> *Counsellor*:   From what you 'see' or 'don't see', is Andrew usually there when your Dad is dismissive of your mother?
>
> *Sue*:   Yeah, I guess that he usually is.

The counsellor in the above dialogue is using the observations of family members not only to frame a description of the event by those people involved but she is also using the person not present to help move towards the clarification of who was present for the interactive sequence.

As this dialogue is developing we are left wondering if mother, father and Andrew would agree that they are all involved and how each of them would see the development of this sequence. Andrew has given the impression that in his view his father is to blame for what happens and its effect on his mother, whereas Susan may not quite agree with that. Possibly between the two children there is difference in the way they 'blame' and see causal mechanisms operating in the family. It may well be that other family members would again have different causal attributions about this event. Certainly if the family is to operate in a coordinated and consistent way their view of what 'starts' things needs to be closely linked, such that they can then take united action to remedy the situation. Here are some questions that our counsellor asks to clarify an element of the situation.

> *Counsellor*: So when these situations occur of your mother blurting things out and your father becoming angry, whose fault do you think it is, Andrew?
>
> *Andrew*: As I said, my father, it's so difficult to approach him.
>
> *Counsellor*: And you, Sue, I know you're not there. Whose fault if anybody's do you think it is?
>
> *Sue*: Well it's a bit difficult but I think Mum handles Dad better when Andrew's not there. She's a little more tentative when he's around.
>
> *Counsellor*: Oh right, so the way she is with your Dad seems different with Andrew there and when he's not?
>
> *Sue*: Yeah, I don't know, I somehow feel she's less bothered by it.
>
> *Counsellor*: OK. Mrs Davies, I'm not sure I understand it all, you know, what Sue says, but do you think anybody is to blame for these kinds of rows?
>
> *Mrs Davies*: Oh well yes, I don't do it right. I suppose it's me you know . . . not knowing how to do it.
>
> *Counsellor*: You sound resigned to that at the moment. [*Mrs Davies*: Mmm, Mmm.] If he were here what would your husband say in reply to that question?
>
> *Mrs Davies*: Oh he'd say it was my fault.
>
> *Andrew*: He sure would.
>
> *Sue*: He'd blame Mum but I'm not sure what he would really think.
>
> *Counsellor*: So there are some differences about explaining how these rows develop?

Because a distinction, a difference in 'whose fault it is', has become apparent, the counsellor here follows the tack of asking the same question of each member of the family and she also asks for their view on how they think Mr Davies would reply. This serves the purpose of being very clear as to who thinks what and thereby laying the foundation for an issue that could profitably be elaborated on. It allows this particular family to know where each stands in relation to this issue and as such provides some structural information about who is close to whom. The benefit of focusing on clarifying distinctions is quite important as families who have been repeating problematic behaviour for a time often have some family members who are holding on to a particular view with too much certainty. This of course means that those family members severely limit their ability to entertain other ways of thinking and behaving and hence their availability to embark on problem solving strategies is limited.

In the above piece of dialogue, many other clarifying questions could be asked. 'What does angry and blurting out mean?' 'How do family members see the son attempt to approach the father?' 'What does Sue mean by difficult – is it just difficult for her to know or is it difficult to voice a different opinion to her brother?' 'When did Sue notice the difference in the way her mother approaches her father – was it before or after Andrew left home?' 'Do other family members agree with Sue?' etc., etc. As always, the curious stance provokes many different possibilities.

Box 6. 2   Clarifying and expanding

The counsellor should:

1   Link levels of meaning.
2   Promote the observer perspective.
3   Ask questions that clarify distinctions.

Opening communication

Family members who say 'The trouble is we do not communicate' and professionals who say 'We have to help them communicate' clearly do not have an interactive perspective. As the adage goes, it is impossible to not communicate. Families that face a problem do communicate. It is just that the nature of their communication is not helpful to them finding a solution to their problem. The communication they embark on will also be repetitive and hence not be generating new information. Families need to be clear about what is being communicated so they can begin to create a context for generating something different. They need to be able to recognize all the interactive elements that play a part in their efforts to solve particular problems and that includes how everyone thinks and feels about that particular problem. In doing this they also need to find ways to give each other suitable messages. The counsellor therefore, in attempting to open communication, should see her activity as oiling a rusty bicycle; the counsellor is engaged in lubricating the family's interaction about the topic at hand.

The most important way in which family members can be helped to consider their interaction about the problem is to encourage them to become aware of their own activity in relation to the activity of others. In becoming better able to inform others about one's own feelings and thoughts, a family member is not only improving their own communicative effectiveness but also encouraging others to do similarly. This process is simply done by asking people how they were thinking and feeling at a particular time, followed by asking them how they believed other family members were thinking and feeling at the same time. Then, by asking similar questions of the other members present in a way that has a natural conversational flow about it, the counsellor acts as a channel aiming to help family members 'hear' the views of everyone. In the early stages of counselling, the family will not 'hear' in the empathic sense, but the counsellor will be ensuring that the clogged channels of the family's communication mechanisms are being slowly and gently unblocked, especially by reflecting feelings and thoughts.

Counsellor: Mrs Davies, when you ask your husband something difficult, what is going through your mind?

Mrs Davies: Oh . . . I'm going to get this wrong. I wish I didn't have to.

Counsellor: What do you think you husband thinks?

Mrs Davies: I don't know really, he's just doing things his way.

Counsellor: And what about your son, what do you think is going on for him?

Mrs Davies: He's just watching, checks it out.

Counsellor: What is happening for you Andrew? Is your Mum right about that?

Andrew: I'm just anticipating Dad getting angry, that's all.

Counsellor: So if I were observing you, you know, sitting there watching it, I was wondering what I would see?

Andrew: Nothing much, I don't say anything but I suppose I would have a look on my face.

Counsellor: A look on your face – what sort of look? How do you think your mother would see it?

Andrew: I suppose she'd think the same. 'He's upset that Dad's going to get angry again'.

Counsellor: So you think your Mum would be aware of you being angry. And what about your father, how do you think he looks on your look?

In this section of dialogue the counsellor is sharing out the **perspectives of 'self' and 'other'** from several individuals. The process of considering the information from or about one individual in the family is important but problems will arise if in the counselling session there is too much focus on a specific individual and there is no sharing out of information about the event from the perspective of others. When one individual provides too much information from his/her own perspective the counsellor needs to clarify whether this is the same information that is communicated at home and in so doing the perspectives of others will be brought into the discussion. Similarly, when several family members focus on one specific individual, that is, when they are over-focused on the 'other', some questions to provoke consideration about 'self' perspectives are necessary.

In the early stages of counselling many of the statements being made by individuals will have been made elsewhere at some time and as such are not novel. At these times the only interaction that will follow in the counselling room will be a repeat of the interaction that occurs at home. The counsellor can take this and build on it by asking whether or not the person has said what they said before, encouraging the 'self' perspective by asking the person to elaborate, encouraging the 'other' perspective by asking how they imagine certain other family members would view their comment. This then stops the familiar 'communication' pattern and encourages the consideration of other elements in its composition. A similar occurrence in the session will be that following some statement from an individual perspective another family member will come in with a comment. The counsellor should allow this spontaneous interaction but it again needs to be recognized that in the early stages of counselling the majority of such interactions tend to be similar to the ones that occur elsewhere. At this point structuring skills will become important in order to create a feeling of safety and prevent the possibility of maladaptive patterns occurring. The counsellor therefore allows the spontaneous interaction as a means to introduce a further element of the interactive chain but also gives the message that each person should have the opportunity to comment on how things are from their own perspective. It is necessary to then comment on the spontaneous interaction and check whether or not it occurs at home, thus indicating that the interaction is seen as a significant event in the session. Family members are then invited also to comment on this event.

> *Counsellor*:   Andrew, and what about your father? How do you think he looks on your look?
>
> *Andrew*:   Well he's not bothered really is he, he just thinks I'm angry all the time.
>
> *Sue*:   You always say that about him but he just doesn't think bad about you. He does have other feelings.
>
> *Andrew*:   Look just because he doesn't treat you that way doesn't mean that he treats me in the same way. It's always been different.
>
> *Counsellor*:   Sue, I'm not sure what you meant by Andrew always saying that.
>
> *Sue*:   Well he's always going on about Dad, not really respecting him and it bothers me that they don't try to get on.
>
> *Counsellor*:   Andrew, what do you feel about Sue saying that?
>
> *Andrew*:   Well I know it's sad but Dad doesn't do anything about it.
>
> *Counsellor*:   It does seem sad doesn't it. I was wondering though, Mrs Davies, how do you feel when Andrew and Sue have words like that?
>
> *Mrs Davies*:   I wish I could stop them. It makes me feel so helpless, all this arguing and I'm not sure what about.
>
> *Counsellor*:   I'm not sure if the words between Andrew and Sue are the same as home – what happens there [*to Mrs Davies*]?
>
> *Mrs Davies*:   Well Andrew comes in after something that may have happened with his father, he slumps down in the chair, all miserable and huffy and Sue comes in and says 'Angry with Dad again?'.
>
> *Counsellor*:   So Andrew's just there with this look on his face and Sue makes a comment about him and his father. Is that how you see them?
>
> *Mrs Davies*:   That's right, they then just argue about him.

In building up the layers of meaning and behaviour, opening communication begins with 'myself as I see me'. It then moves to 'other individuals as I see them'. As the counsellor is asking each individual about other family members, the next layer is 'me as others see me' and this is built up from listening to the replies to the counsellor's questions to others. The next layer is 'me relating to person A as person B sees us'. This again comes from listening this time to the perspective of one person about interaction that two other people are involved in ('Mrs Davies, how do you feel when Andrew and Sue have words like that?'). Tomm (1987) has labelled the type of questioning that permits the development of this awareness as **triadic questioning**, that is, questions which explore the interactions that do not include the person being addressed, thus enabling this (third) person to become more of an observer. We see this type of question in the last statement of the counsellor above. The importance of triadic questioning is twofold:

it allows the interacting couple to observe how their interaction is observed by 'others' and it secondly rapidly educates family members that each of them can and is able to comment on the interactions of any other set of individuals in the family because they are automatically involved in it even when merely observing. This process of realizing that one's behaviour is being observed and that one can observe 'others' including 'me as seen by others' is the origin of the freeing up of the 'communication' with the family. It serves to make each individual reflect on their position in the interactive system and that reflection may indeed lead to some behaviour change.

Box 6. 3   Opening communication

The counsellor should:

1   Encourage 'self' awareness.
2   Encourage 'other' awareness.
3   Share out perspectives among individuals.
4   Allow spontaneous interactions.
5   Ask triadic questions.
6   Invite comment on significant events.

Breaking maladaptive patterns

Families with problems repeat the same interaction over and over. It is as if they have a set dance and each family will 'dance their dance' if given the opportunity to do so. For each problem they will have developed over time a particular way of dealing with each other. Each will have their own assigned role and each will play it to the full whenever the sequence is started. When these maladaptive patterns occur within sessions they can result in family members feeling that the whole counselling process is hopeless, and hence when they occur repeatedly they can seriously undermine the hope that counselling engenders. Being able to intervene in a meaningful way with these interactive patterns is a skill that is very much part of the general skill of structuring. In essence the counsellor's task is to stop the repetitive process and then analyse what happens in terms of the interactions and associated feelings and thoughts. The counsellor should then explore some alternative ways of considering that particular interactive event.

As the family 'problem' is expressed through a maladaptive pattern, the family's experience of this pattern will be one of frustration, anger, anxiety and usually some element of resignation. Family members are aware that the interactions around the pattern are unhelpful but typically each will experience the behaviour of other members as unhelpful while viewing their own as meaningfully attempting to solve the problem. Families need to experience the situation in which the counsellor has been able to tolerate, contain and confront them as they 'dance their dance'. This is achieved by being able directly to stop the interaction, not in a commanding or overbearing way, but in a manner that seems to insist that a particular question be answered at that time. The counsellor then intervenes by moving the family away from the repetitive interactions on to a discussion about the interaction. This is another version of the counselling process that offers family members the opportunity to observe their own interaction. This can best be achieved by asking someone to comment on what has just happened in the room. The counsellor in effect takes charge of the problematic interaction by inviting family members to talk about it and naturally in the discussion that follows she will be demonstrating her ability to deal with the emotions that are a feature of the particular interaction.

When there are young children involved in the session they may misbehave, in these circumstances the counsellor needs to be more forceful in stopping this behaviour. Statements such as 'I don't think it's a good idea to let him continue to behave like that while we are trying to discuss these things' can and should have the desired result. However when such a 'misbehaviour' event does occur the counsellor needs to be observant about two important aspects. First, the emotional theme and content, just prior to the child's misbehaviour, should be noted. This is because it is not unusual for children to misbehave whenever a difficult issue is discussed and if this does seem to occur repeatedly then it should be commented on. Secondly, the parents' handling of the child during one of these incidents should be followed closely for it may have implications as to how they handle other issues; of course often when young children are present the general theme tends to be one of parenting and the parents' handling of the child can then become the focus of the counselling itself.

In the example we are pursuing, however, young children are not involved but the last segment of dialogue did suggest that Mrs Davies let her grown-up children simply get on with it. A potential process-interrupting question is demonstrated in the next segment.

Andrew: But Mum have you thought why we argue. It's you, you just won't stand up to him [*Mrs Davies looks down: Sue looks the other way*]. Every time it's the same. You need to do something about it. Why do you let it go on for so long? Well . . . [*waits for reply*] . . . I just don't understand you, you put up with so much and don't you even think . . . I don't know why I try so hard to make . . .

Counsellor: [*extends her hand to Andrew with a slow down motion but looks at Mrs Davies*] Mrs Davies, Andrew seems angry at this moment. Does this happen at home?

Mrs Davies: Yes I suppose it does.

Counsellor: And just as I saw here, do you just remain quiet?

Mrs Davies: Well, it's the way I do things – it's what he's complaining about.

The counsellor has been able to stop Andrew's tirade towards his mother and she has elicited from Mrs Davies some comments about her behaviour. The family need to be able to experience this obvious repeating event in a different manner, and to begin to do that they need to be able to describe what happened. The counsellor therefore asks of family members that they provide their description of the event.

Counsellor: Andrew, what did you see happening there, you know, when you got angry?

Andrew: Well it's Mum, she just won't stand . . .

Counsellor: Yes I appreciate you feel your mother doesn't stand up for herself. What I wanted to know was how *you saw* what just happened – you know, from your perspective?

Andrew: Well Mum seemed to be blaming us for arguing and I wanted to tell her I thought she could do things different and well . . . ? I'm not sure.

Counsellor: What did you notice your mother do?

Andrew: She just becomes quiet, backed off . . . like.

Counsellor: And your sister?

Andrew: Had a fed-up look and withdrew.

Counsellor: So you felt that something was not quite fair, you got angry, Mum becomes quiet and Sue withdraws. Is that what everyone saw? [*Mrs Davies and Sue both nod.*]

Having a clear interactive description of this process the family need to be helped further by examining the feelings and thoughts that are associated with this process. In particular there needs to be some exploration of individuals' intentions about what they did and why. Each individual will have determined long ago his or her version of the expected consequences of their behaving differently and the way for the counsellor to encourage new ways of behaving is to have each family member clear about his or her intentions and the intentions of other family members. As the feelings in these repetitive processes tend to be intense and often extreme, individuals will often feel threatened by the possibility of exposure to the feelings of others. Therefore this process is worth being considered as one of confrontation and the counsellor will be using her skills of containing intense emotion to have the family deal with this.

On some occasions family members will give big signals, both verbally and non-verbally, that this issue perhaps should not be discussed because it is a difficult one for them, but the counsellor needs to be gently persistent about this.

> *Counsellor*: Andrew, you know you seemed very angry about that. What in particular led to you feeling like that?
> *Andrew*: Well I'm angry with my Dad 'cos he makes it so difficult and well . . .
> *Counsellor*: I can see that, I was wondering about your feelings to your Mum?
> *Andrew*: Well yes, of course I am angry at her. You see she does nothing and well, she doesn't listen to me. I say these things and it's like banging my head against a brick wall because she doesn't seem to listen.
> *Counsellor*: So you feel somewhat discounted because she doesn't seem to take any notice. Does that make it worse?
> *Andrew*: Yeah, it sure does. I don't know which I'm angriest about in the end.
> *Counsellor*: And you, Mrs Davies, what do you feel when Andrew is angry with you like that?
> *Mrs Davies*: I do listen to him, he has got important things to say. It's not right, he shouldn't feel like that.
> *Counsellor*: Right, I understand that you sympathize with him but you're telling me what you think about Andrew's feelings. What I'm really wanting to know is how do you feel when he shouts at you like he did.
> *Mrs Davies*: I get those sad feelings, you know like I can't get it right for any of them and well [*Counsellor encourages: Mmm, mmm*] I feel got at. I'm always wrong and they all find a way of making sure I know it.

Having reached this particular point, the counsellor has a number of alternatives. She could ask Andrew what he feels about what his mother has just said; she could remain quiet and see what spontaneous interactions occur or she could make a more active intervention. Although a number of interventions could be appropriate at this point, a particularly useful one with maladaptive patterns is to have family members explore the exact opposite in meaning and context from that which occurred. In terms of the exact opposite, the counsellor would take major feelings or thoughts by the participants in this event, which in this case are 'not listened to' and 'angry' in Andrew's case and 'sad' and 'got at' by Mrs Davies. One would then choose the polar opposites 'listened to', 'not angry', 'happy' and 'left alone' and then find a means of introducing these into a question. In essence this is to counteract the tendency for the family to become locked into seeing events in a particular set way and consequently limiting their options for behavioural change. A few well chosen questions from an opposite viewpoint could begin to free them from their constricted cognitive set and hence begin to raise the opportunity of new possibilities. In our case the counsellor could ask what it is like when Mrs Davies and Andrew are together and Andrew is not angry or what does Mrs Davies do with Andrew when she is happy. However, the session does not quite proceed along these lines:

> *Counsellor*:   Are there times when you, Andrew, say something to your mother and you, Mrs Davies, feel that you listen to him? [*Mrs Davies and Andrew look at each other quizzically.*]
>
> *Andrew*:   Not so much now I'm not at home . . . I suppose colours in the house, you know when they are decorating.
>
> *Mrs Davies*:   Yes, Andrew is talented in knowing what colour goes with what room. When we did our decorating, well his Dad and I both asked him for his opinion then.
>
> *Counsellor*:   That sounds as if that worked well.
>
> *Mrs Davies*:   I suppose so.
>
> *Counsellor*:   Well it tells us that if you value Andrew's opinion, he knows how to give it to you and you know how to take it.
>
> *Mrs Davies*:   Oh yes, I really respect his talent with colours.
>
> *Counsellor*:   Its good when families can do things well together like that. [*Everyone smiles at each other.*] But unfortunately with this problem – you know when arguments occur – I was wondering what would happen, Mrs Davies, if afterwards, people just, well, if they just left you alone?
>
> *Mrs Davies*:   How do you mean, if when my husband is angry and isn't bothered, that the kids just left me alone? [*Counsellor nods.*] Oh, it would let me get on of course. Do what I need to do.
>
> *Counsellor*:   That's an advantage. Any disadvantages if you were left alone?
>
> *Mrs Davies*:   Well, when Andrew gets involved like that I suppose I know that he's bothered – it shows he's bothered about me.

By examining an opposite context we find that the counsellor has been able to identify that Mrs Davies and Andrew are aware of a set of circumstances when Andrew offers his opinion constructively and his mother is able to listen. This interaction is clearly in direct contrast to the maladaptive pattern. The counsellor makes the choice of not directly pointing out this but instead focuses on supporting positive elements in the reported interaction. The counsellor uses the fact of the presence of positives to return rapidly to the difficult interaction. It is as if the counsellor uses the positive as a stepping stone in travelling through the family's problem. The counsellor returns to the problem not only because there was a brief respite but also to demonstrate to the family that they have a flexible approach. Families struggling with a difficult repeating interaction have a tendency to cling on to a new conception immediately it is offered and to hold on to that just as rigidly. In our example it would be very easy for the family to assume that the problem has arisen because Andrew wants to give an opinion when it is not required and hence the solution would obviously be Andrew's responsibility to shut up. If this is the only alternative offered it plays into the blaming mechanism in the family. By immediately considering a number of other contexts the counsellor can prevent this process and provide the family with the experience of a range of possibilities that are within their repertoire of behaviour.

Box 6.4 Breaking maladaptive patterns

The counsellor should:

1 Interrupt the unhelpful/repetitive process.
2 Help the family describe the unhelpful process.
3 Confront intentions and feelings in the unhelpful process.
4 Explore opposite context and meaning.

Linking past, present and future

Families with problems are often so focused on present difficulties or on past history that they function in a way as if there is no future. Tomorrow is experienced as just a repeat of today. Such an orientation provides a paucity of problem solving strategies, as no alternative ways of behaviour are considered. At the other extreme are families who are so fearful of particular events happening in the future that they live their present life seemingly in an endless task of preventing those events from occurring. Again such is the over-focus on a particular time frame that the development of a range of present day behaviour is severely hampered. The counsellor therefore has to investigate the way the family considers its present day behaviour in terms of the past or future and this is not only done to bring to awareness the domination of another time over the present, it is also done in order to elaborate on past or future events which the family have not considered in a search for a solution. Each family will have some hidden or neglected strengths in their history and similarly a more reflexive view of the future could also unearth possibilities that may be considered beneficial.

In terms of her investigation into the family's time continuum, the counsellor should bear in mind that each family, broadly speaking, will categorize time for themselves into three past periods and two future. These being:

1   **Historical time.** This is the time which in an intact family is before the adult couple came together. It includes all those relationships observed as a child, particularly the one between his/her parents. It will also cover those adult relationships of family members which have ceased, that is, previous partners and marriages. The importance of this time is that it may well contain patterns of relating which dominate the present or which potentially could offer alternatives to present day relating. Family members need to be helped in feeling linked to the positive but psychologically separated from the negative elements of their family's history.

2   **'Before' time.** Families can readily refer to a time before the problem emerged. This may be the time before the major illness, before the handicap child was born, before the husband had the affair, before a particular developmental stage was reached. For some people this 'before' time refers to some halcyon days when everything worked very well. The need is realistically to appraise family functioning at this 'before' time in order to prevent the scapegoating of the person who is the identified problem as well as utilizing useful family interaction that may have withered away. Many families completely forget the 'before' thus losing or masking positives and strengths as this time has not been allowed to affect the present. Here the counsellor will be attempting to retrieve this time so that its beneficial qualities may be applied to the present.

3   **Last week.** This is the period of time just prior to the session and most likely the atmosphere present at the beginning of the session will largely be determined by 'last week'. Frequently, however, the whole history of the problem may seem to be defined solely in terms of 'last week'. Families tend to respond to the recent past as if it were a continuation of how the problem has been for some while. Each family will need to review 'last week' in realistic terms so that the idea of the problem can be seen as having a change element through time,

for if change in past time can be demonstrated then change in future time is also likely.

4 **Next week.** Nearly all families will see 'next week' as being potentially different from 'last week'. Once a realistic description of what transpired 'last week' has occurred, then it becomes very useful to juxtapose that with questions about what may happen next week. Again, if in the process of reflexive questioning a family acquires a sense of a problem being variable through time, then straightforwardly asking 'What will you do next week?' spontaneously introduces the notion of choice within a context that may change. One particular category of questioning that is important about 'next week' is that which deals with expectations individuals may have about events following what has transpired in the counselling session itself. For example, if two people have argued in the session or a family member has said something for the first time, the question would be 'Since that happened here today, what do you think will happen about it when you get home or in the next day or two?'. Here the counsellor is clearly making links between the present and immediate future so that family members can communicate openly about events in their family and point out the process of change 'between sessions' as having an importance.

5 **The future.** Thoughts about the future can to a considerable extent determine present behaviour. Whether the future inappropriately dominates current action or whether the family do not consider it at all the counsellor does need to ensure that the distant future is seen as having a role in the present situation. Even though the asking about future eventualities may not produce much in the verbal output of family members, this certainly is a category of question that family members take home with them and work at in their own way. First the counsellor needs to confront the negative view of the future in terms of asking about the potential outcome if the problem remains. 'If your son and husband continue to argue, what do you think will happen?' This can then be extended into a catastrophic expectation question: 'If you don't manage to do something about this difficulty, what is the very worst thing that could happen?' Of course, in families where the executive subsystem agrees about the catastrophic expectation counselling will, for some little while, proceed differently from when the executive subsystem disagrees; in the latter case, clarifying of the differences will be important. Another type of questioning concerns the exploration of hypothetical possibilities; here the

counsellor constructs a scenario which may or may not have some possibility of occurring and questions family members about how such an event would unfold. 'Mrs Davies, supposing you and your daughter were out when your son called. How do you think he and his father would get on then?' 'Supposing your son became very ill, what do you think his father would do then?' The type of future-orientated question that leads naturally into identifying problem solving strategies are those that ask about future goals. 'What plans do you have for dealing with this situation next time it arises?' 'If everybody was willing, what help do you think you need to tackle this problem?' Future-orientation questions are also necessary as they clearly imply that the future belongs to the family. It is their responsibility, with the counsellor playing no role.

The counsellor therefore may range freely in the way in which she deals with past and future time. All the while, however, she will be attempting to be mindful of the 'Now' dimension, for one of the aims of counselling will be to assist individuals to experience the present unfettered by past prejudices and future worries. Even if only one individual in a family can improve this ability to be located in the here and now, this in itself will have many repercussions for how the family will be able to problem solve when difficulties emerge. As Rogers (1967) pointed out, if one person is congruent in terms of feelings and awareness then that person's communication will be clear, encouraging others to respond with clarity.

To return to the Davies' family session:

Counsellor: I know you feel that Andrew is bothered about you and that you're not certain about your husband. Has there been a time when he was bothered – you know, in a general way?

Mrs Davies: Well yes, when we were first married and then when the children were much younger, everything was OK then.

Counsellor: It was easier for him and you then?

Mrs Davies: Yes it was.

Counsellor: So when did it seem as if your husband wasn't bothered?

Mrs Davies: Perhaps gradually. The children got older, I started work, Andrew left home and the last couple of months since his job finished.

Counsellor: So he changed over that time . . . Do you think he would say that you have changed over that time too? The children have obviously changed, growing up and all that. How do you think your husband would say you've changed?

Mrs Davies: Oh I'm not sure. I suppose I get on with my own things more. He'd probably say something like that – I'm not around to look after him more.

Counsellor: OK. So at one time his 'bothering' was fine when you were more tied to the family. Now you're not, he's out of work and this difficulty is around. Supposing you go home after today and you tell him that, you know what I've just said, what would you expect him to say?

Mrs Davies: He might not say much at all or perhaps agree, say it was my fault for not bothering with him.

Counsellor: And if he said that what would you say?

Mrs Davies: Nothing, I just don't get involved with that. I'd go off.

Counsellor: I guess that would just indicate that you're not bothered by that kind of discussion at all.

Mrs Davies: That's right, yes, it doesn't get anywhere.

Counsellor: I was wondering, in the not too distant future, your children will leave and life will again be different. Have you had any ideas how this thing might work out – have you any plans about how you and your husband may go back to how it was before the children?

Mrs Davies: I've not really thought about it really.

Apart from historical time, the counsellor has taken Mrs Davies through the time continuum, not really dwelling on any particular time. Clearly some skills of successful 'bothering' were present in the past and the context has been extended to include a situation when the term 'not bothered' can be applied to Mrs Davies. It is also apparent that there is little future orientation. Time that is to come at the moment merely represents an extension of the present.

Box 6.5 Linking past, present and future

The counsellor should ask about:

1 Historical time.
2 'Before' time.
3 Last week.
4 Next week.
5 The future.

Imparting information

All families construct theories to explain certain events and experiences. With repeating difficulties these theories come to dominate how family members respond to particular behaviours. Sometimes a behaviour can be within the normal limits that one would expect of a person of that developmental stage in that context, but the family fail to see it in this way and they may have constructed an idiosyncratic response to it as a consequence. Families vary in the extent to which they believe themselves to be different from others and it is a common occurrence for individuals and families to feel that they are abnormal when they encounter a common difficulty. As this occurs quite frequently, there are typical myths which feed the idiosyncratic theories that families have about particular problems. A selection of these myths being:

- If you are caring for a chronically ill or handicapped person you should do this willingly and happily and not experience any difficult emotions.
- If a chronically ill or handicapped person expresses any negative thoughts or feelings, this is because they do not 'accept' their condition.
- Whenever someone who is chronically sick, handicapped or a child behaves in a difficult manner, there is always a reason for this which is to do with the extent they wish to 'get at' the carers.
- All children should behave at all times and if they do not, they should respond to reasoned arguments.
- Negative feelings in one family member are always caused by another family member.

The list could go on, but it is relatively simple to appreciate how such notions can interfere with a family's problem solving ability. Coupled with the self-pathologizing tendency in families, quite normative behaviour could therefore be seen as being a problem. Also behaviour that is only minimally problematic can remain increasingly so as the family have no knowledge of the normative path the behaviour could in fact take.

Families therefore need help in being clear about behaviour that can reasonably be expected to occur in a particular context. The normative dimension is therefore one that has considerable bearing on reponses to traumatic events, child management strategies and the care of individuals with chronic illness and handicap. Rolland (1984, 1987) has outlined a framework for understanding the psychosocial implications of chronic illness on the family life and in doing so has indicated the predictable transitions and feelings that occur. With such a framework in place, it becomes possible to place the family's experience within a normative context. Similarly many families fail to take into account usual and expected childhood and adult reactions to family events and hence come to pathologize behaviour which when placed in a developmentally appropriate framework becomes understandable. In such circumstances the counsellor's task will be to offer information that directs the family towards appropriate expectations.

In presenting this information, the counsellor does not wish to imply to the family that they are 'getting it wrong'. What is required is the gentle clarification of their view of the problem and then the asking of questions which invite family members to consider a normative comparison. Questions such as 'How much do you think this is typical of people with multiple sclerosis?' or 'To what extent do you think her behaviour is the same as other 10-year-olds?' or 'How much do you think she behaves like that because she is in a wheelchair or because she's an average 16-year-old?' or 'What do you think is the usual emotional reaction when a man loses his job?'. In effect the counsellor is inviting the family to consider how much they are meeting 'normal' occurrences and therefore is utilizing their desire to be the same as other people.

The other means of testing how information would be received is in another variety of the 'what if' question. 'What would you say if I told you that in my experience . . .' with the counsellor making some statement about the normative element of the behaviour. It is important for the counsellor to stress her own experience as being the authority for the normative statement simply because she cannot say 'I read a book last week and I expect you to take my word on trust'. Clients need to feel that the information they are to be given flows directly from the counsellor's experience of their specific problem and that it is not just a matching of signs and symptoms to some average formula. Families need to experience the counsellor being involved with their problem before they can begin to accept any information that allows them to make changes.

The method that is being advocated here is one that fits very well with family interviews in which the interviewer has the ultimate aim of presenting some new factual information to the client. Following the initial phase of the session, the interviewer who examines the family's understanding of the topic and issues at hand utilizes the skills outlined in the previous chapter. From that position she then would need to clarify those areas that the family have some certainty about and those where they feel confused. At that point some normative comparison questions can be asked and, given the family's responses, the interviewer could identify those areas where the family do not need information, those areas where they seem to be asking for information and those areas where it may be beneficial if they have more information. All individuals are far more attentive and able to take in new information if they feel they have been heard, their feelings acknowledged and their views understood. Whenever new information may have emotional consequences, it can only effectively be imparted within the containment and the acceptance of counselling. This cannot be neglected in the provision of care to those families having to deal with disease and disability. Some imparting information examples are described below.

1   Some divorcing parents consider the upset their children show to be unusual or unnatural. Typical childhood reactions to divorce have been well described by Robinson (1991). Research has also demonstrated that divorce does produce negative effects in the short term. These effects diminish over time and the children are eventually better adjusted than those who remain within discordant families (Hetherington and Clingempeel, 1992).

2   Families in which a member has a major affective disorder have been helped to prevent relapse by family members being instructed in methods that reduce negatively expressed emotions, the principle method essentially being an educational approach that informs families of the stressful impact of negative emotions on their 'patient' member (Anderson et al., 1985).

3   Gilhooly (1987), in discussing the impact of senile dementia on the family, notes how carers lacking knowledge about the condition can lead to troubling behaviours being interpreted as deliberate provocations by the dependent person. She reports on a study which demonstrated that providing written information about the condition showed significant improvement in the distress felt by family carers. The information was considered beneficial in that it allowed the carer to reframe difficult behaviour as being illness-related.

The Davies family session continues:

Counsellor: How typical do you think Andrew's behaviour is in coming home and staying so often? You know, for a 21-year-old with a flat.

Mrs Davies: Well I suppose it does seem a lot. I wouldn't not like to see him but he does seem to stay a lot.

Counsellor: My experience tells me that it's OK for someone who has moved out to visit every so often but it's not quite usual for them to stay so frequently.

Mrs Davies: No, I wouldn't think so.

Counsellor: How might we help you and Andrew with that? Perhaps it should be one thing or the other, you know, live at home or in a flat.

Andrew: Well I don't want to come back to live.

Sue: So don't come home so often.

Counsellor: I'm not sure saying it like that is helpful. I am wondering how your parents and he can be helped to get it so it's like most young people.

The session is now on the theme that the counsellor considered as being potentially important when she framed a view of the family's stage in the life cycle. Themes of this nature are often introduced into the session by the counsellor asking a normative comparison question. In this piece of dialogue, perhaps because the counsellor now feels she knows the family well enough and that she has given them opportunity to feel that they have been heard she feels able to offer a normative piece of information. It is of interest in what follows that the counsellor maintains a balanced view to potential solutions in that she indicates that help could be given to live at home or in a flat. The counsellor is therefore not giving the message it is unusual for this to happen, therefore the son needs to stay away; her message is that it is somewhat unusual, perhaps things could change. We therefore move on to problem solving strategies.

7

Problem Solving Strategies

Take no thought of the harvest
But only of proper sowing.

T.S. Eliot

Identifying strategies

In identifying problem solving strategies there are three general
dimensions to consider.

1   Family expectations.
2   The one solution hope.
3   The family structure and decision making process.

Family expectations

As the session continues it will be necessary for the counsellor to
begin to identify problem solving strategies bearing in mind the
expectations the family had of counselling. This is because those
families that clearly expected the counsellor to offer 'advice and
guidance' will be expecting and anticipating more activity on the
part of the counsellor than those families who just expect to talk
about the problem. In many respects the counsellor's activity may
show little difference with each of these families but her general
interactive style with each will be different so as to meet expectations. Thus with those families expecting more activity the
counsellor may say, 'Well we're coming to a time when we need to
work out exactly what to do. It would help me in my task if . . .'
and then continue questioning, whereas the counsellor with the
'let's talk' family will do just that, simply talk, almost identifying
problem solving strategies in passing.

The one solution hope

In trying to identify problem solving strategies the counsellor
should be wary of attempting to find one strategy that will for
once and for all eliminate the difficulty the family have. This

simply is the counsellor's equivalent of the family's 'magic wand' scenario. Problem solving strategies should be seen as producing 'transitional' outcomes, that is, outcomes that are on the way to the belief that matters are concluded, whatever that turns out to be. As we have seen in Chapter 1, the concept of transition refers to a period of time of interim arrangements which follows or precedes a period of greater stability. In terms of helping families find solutions to their ongoing difficulties it is important to give the message that as life is constantly changing then the need to establish solutions to difficulties is a constant one. The solution that will eliminate problems for ever does not exist. The importance of dealing with difficulties lies in the process of solving a problem, not in the solution itself − solutions of necessity can and do change but the process of arriving at a solution has a validity that continues through time and therefore needs to be enhanced. Each solution is therefore not only 'transitional' in terms of the process in the family through time; solutions are also 'transitional' in the family processes throughout the course of counselling. Families therefore need to appreciate that any solution achieved is just a step on the path, the path towards the experience of satisfactory functioning. Sometimes when families arrive for counselling with clear-cut goals they often become confused about the counselling process when they adopt solutions that have beneficial outcomes but do not seem very related to their 'goal'. When this happens they can be uncertain about continuing with counselling, because some sense of improvement is felt, but they are aware of not having achieved their goals. The review of goals in the light of the actual experience of counselling needs to be an ongoing and continual process.

The family structure and decision making process

It should not be assumed that everyone in the family is of equal importance in the framing of and agreeing a problem solving strategy. In order for families to function effectively, parents should effectively be in charge of young people; adolescence should be dealt with with respect but with clarity and firmness about the rules and obligations that apply to them. Adult children and relatives, including the elderly, need to appreciate the difference between consultation and decision making in negotiating with the persons in the family who ultimately decide on the strategy to be followed. To put it simply, the executive subsystem of the family needs to be recognized and given its own appropriate authority within family sessions. Of course, in an instance where another family member is inappropriately involved in the parental/marital executive subsystem then some transitional steps may need to be taken to eliminate that involvement. In most cases, however, the family will automatically follow the counsellor's lead when she deals with the executive subsystem in a way that is respectful and appropriate.

In moving towards identifying problem solving strategies, the counsellor should link the family's process of making changes in the past with the change process that hopefully is to come. Initially this is done by finding out the strategies family members have attempted in the past. There are several reasons for doing this. First, the family's usual mechanism of solving problems needs to be understood by all. Secondly, the family need to feel that they have embarked on some problem solving earlier and that this had good elements as well as encountering difficulties. Thirdly, the family need to identify with the counsellor those 'factors' which they see as blocking solutions. Finally, the counsellor needs to have a good appreciation of what failed and why so that she does not go on and simply make suggestions which merely repeat the family's history. In terms of the latter, it is always worth remembering the adage, if 'common sense' could have solved it, it would not be a problem.

The means of **identifying previous solutions** is simply to ask 'What have you attempted in the past to sort out this problem?'. This will become an expanded version of what occurred when the family was met initially, but some major differences are present. In asking about previous solutions it is always helpful not to inquire about previous attempts to sort out the actual initial problem as presented by the family. So, in the case of the Davies family, one would not inquire of Mrs Davies 'What have you done in the past to stop feeling stressed so that your diabetes is more in control?'. To do this would clearly begin the blaming process or, in this case, the self-blaming process of Mrs Davies. 'They are expecting me to have done something about it and I haven't.' Past solution questions on the initial problem also tend to reinforce the scapegoating mechanisms in the family. The requirement therefore is to ask questions of issues that are only related and linked to the presenting problem. Again, this serves to emphasize the transitional nature of any solution and the interactive nature of the problem.

> *Counsellor*: Mrs Davies, I can see the problem it causes you when Andrew and Sue argue. Have you done anything in the past to stop it from happening?
> *Mrs Davies*: At the beginning I used to ask them politely after it was over.

Counsellor: Was that both of them together or separately?

Mrs Davies: Oh separately, you know quietly, not to do it.

Counsellor: So after it was over you'd find some time to say something to both of them about it?

Mrs Davies: Yes, that's right.

Counsellor: When you did that how did they respond?

Mrs Davies: 'Sorry Mum', 'it's the other's fault', 'won't do it again'.

Counsellor: Both the same? [*Mrs Davies nods.*] What happened then?

Mrs Davies: Well nothing changed so I tried to stop the argument as it was happening.

Counsellor: Do you know why your first line of attack didn't work?

Mrs Davies: I thought it was because they didn't want to stop.

As the discussion continues on this theme we see the counsellor clarifying and tracking interaction and clearly on this particular theme there is a lot of ground to cover.

The next related questions concern solutions that individuals may have considered but have not attempted. Usually these solutions are things that individuals have thought privately and have not been shared with others. Such questions may be seemingly quite benign, in that they simply add some more descriptive information which adds to the opening communication process.

Counsellor: Sue, have you thought to yourself of any way you might stop arguing with Andrew?

Sue: Not really, only to stay out of his way.

Counsellor: What about you, Andrew. Have you thought how you could stop arguing with Sue?

Andrew: The same really. Not get in her way.

Counsellor: So you both think the only solution is not to get involved with each other?

Should any individual indicate that they have thought of a solution that has not been tried, it is important to clarify the reasons why not. It is particularly important to clarify what family members see as being the advantages and disadvantages of such a solution. However, there is a class of questions within this category that are important in that they often serve to bring to the fore difficult emotions. These are questions in which the counsellor herself considers that an extreme solution could be applied to the situation and then asks an individual if he or she has ever thought about it as a solution. Such extreme actions usually involve someone leaving the family, and include separation and divorce, having a child live somewhere else, having a chronic sick or handicapped person be cared for by someone else or having an elderly relative go to live in a residential facility. In all families, about all kinds of problems, there usually is a fantasy entertained by someone that the family would be better off if it did not contain a certain person. This fantasy, which is fearful to the thinker, needs to be directly confronted in family counselling for unfortunately, ultimately, it may be the solution individuals are drifting towards and it may be a realistic solution that will contain benefits for all. The need to confront this is because typically one family member will entertain the extreme solution as a distinct possibility and other members will, if they consider it at all, only consider it as something to be frightened of and hence not for general discussion. Thus the extreme solution is not available for the family's open communication. The counsellor's task is therefore to bring the issue into everyone's awareness and explore the responses and the feelings of everyone.

Sometimes it may be necessary for the counsellor to lead into the 'extreme solution' by introducing the humorous over-the-top extreme solution. This then paves the way for the now seemingly more reasonable extreme solution which is fearfully held.

> *Counsellor*: Have you ever thought of buying a gun and shooting these two, Mrs Davies?
> *Mrs Davies*: Well it had crossed my mind. [*Laughs*] I guess it would be nice.
> *Counsellor*: Have you ever thought of banning Andrew from coming home?
> *Mrs Davies*: Oh yes, I've thought about that all right but well . . . I've thought when Sue leaves home I shall make sure they visit on different days. Anything to keep them apart.
> *Counsellor*: And what do you think would happen if you did bar Andrew? How would you feel?
> *Mrs Davies*: I'd be sad. In fact I think everybody would.
> *Counsellor*: It would be a difficult thing for you to do.

It is essential with these questions that the counsellor follow through with empathic responses, for the extreme solution often taps into the difficult emotions which lie just beneath the surface. If the counsellor decides to continue with this theme it will be useful to focus on the emotional aspect rather than the practical element.

> *Counsellor*: As you all would be sad about that, how would people talk to each other?
> *Mrs Davies*: I don't think we'd be very good about that, we'd be more angry.
> *Counsellor*: How do you mean?
> *Mrs Davies*: Well . . . I . . . Oh I don't know.
> *Sue*: I think Mum means that it's easier to tell somebody you're angry than tell them you're sad.
> *Counsellor*: Is that right . . . you know, if your husband were sad about not having Andrew around then he wouldn't let you know he was sad?

Mrs Davies: That's right, he'd find something to be angry about.
Counsellor: And if you told him you were sad?
Mrs Davies: He'd pooh-pooh me, just not be bothered.
Counsellor: And if you told him you were angry?
Mrs Davies: Oh I wouldn't do that, we'd then just end up arguing.

Here we observe how the extreme solution question has very rapidly touched on the interactions around a difficult emotional theme. There has been a rapid movement from inclusion elements to intimacy elements. The counsellor has to acknowledge the difficult emotions connected with such solutions in this way, for it serves to acknowledge the emotional background against which the family members will evaluate any problem strategy. When the counsellor enters into emotional areas following an extreme solution question, the desire to maintain the discussion at the emotional level for long should be resisted, as to do so would be threatening for the family. These questions can, if put carefully, expose the family's 'weak points' and to overly maintain an interest in these points early in any counselling contact can result in defensive reactions. In our example here, Mrs Davies may feel under threat about how she deals with her husband and this could result in her constructing unhelpful expectations about the counsellor's task. The emotional difficulty has to be correctly identified and contained by the counsellor and then she needs to return to the search for the problem solving strategy. Future opportunities to discuss the emotional themes will undoubtedly arise and, having been introduced in the counselling session, it becomes easier to maintain a focus on them on the second or third occasion they arise. It is also helpful for such themes to appear spontaneously two or three times as this gives the counsellor the opportunity of using that fact in constructing a new task for counselling.

Nearly all families require some help in framing possible solutions and the counsellor may find it necessary to find ways of making suggestions to them. A strategy for offering a solution without making it seem too much like a direct suggestion is the **embedded suggestion question**. In this situation the counsellor aims to point the family in a direction that may prove useful and does this by asking a variant of the 'what if' question; such questions can be asked about actions or beliefs.

Counsellor: Obviously there are a lot of difficult feelings behind this situation but what do you think would happen if you suggested to Andrew that he ration the amount of time he spends in the house?
Mrs Davies: I haven't . . . well . . . what would you think? [*to Andrew*]

Andrew: I don't know, I . . . well it's OK but it could make things difficult for me.

Sue: He means he'd have to do his own washing.

Counsellor: Well a lot of things may need to be negotiated about that . . .

The tone of the counsellor's voice and the choice of particular words can make a considerable difference to the degree to which the suggestion is embedded and the likelihood of family interaction following it. If the question is asked in a very loose way ('I just had a vague thought then, supposing you and Sue went out when Andrew and father were there') then the client may merely have an 'Oh I don't know about that' answer, which does not open discussion in the session and does not really spark the reflexive process. The tone of the question therefore needs to be definite enough to have family members at least hold it within their minds for a while but not too definite so that the question almost ceases to become a question but is in fact the next best thing to a clear suggestion.

Embedded suggestion questions are not confined to the 'What if X happened' variety. They can be used very powerfully by the counsellor internally constructing an image of a different inter-active sequence for the family and then asking a question that implies that interaction. The counsellor is therefore suggesting the interactive sequence as a possibility by posing the question. Again, with our continuing example the counsellor may consider that the children could apologize to Mrs Davies for how they behave and the straightforward embedded suggestion question would be 'What if the children apologized to you?'. Whereas by asking 'Supposing one or both of the children apologized, would you be able to accept such an apology gracefully?' the counsellor is embedding the suggestion about how to accept an apology while the apology is also being suggested. Should Mrs Davies confine her answer solely to her own reaction, this would have implications for how Andrew and Sue think about the possibility of themselves offering an apology.

Counsellor: I was wondering Mrs Davies, supposing Andrew invited you and your husband to visit him, would it be OK for you and your husband to go?

Mrs Davies: It would depend on how it was organized. It would have to be me that made it happen. He might come . . . under some sufferance I suppose [*tentatively*] . . . I would have to ask him with that in my mind.

Counsellor: Supposing Andrew asked your husband directly, you know, without you being around?

Mrs Davies: That type of thing doesn't happen so I'm not sure.
Counsellor: And supposing it did happen, what would you think about it Sue . . . just your mother and father going?

The value of these embedded suggestion questions lies not only in the way in which suggestions can be made and reflected on but also in how they allow the counsellor and the family to experiment. If such a 'suggestion' is clearly not acceptable to some family members, then their immediate reaction to the question will indicate that unacceptability. The counsellor will have put the question in the 'Let's brain storm' mode to prevent herself from being accused of making poor suggestions. By ranging around possible alternatives with such questions the counsellor can eliminate some directions and establish others in the process of looking for change.

Once a family appear to be considering a possible direction to make a change, the counsellor then needs carefully to examine the effects of such a change on all family members. At this point the counsellor becomes the person in the counselling system who has the role of maintaining a view of everyone's interests. As solutions seem to suggest themselves it is all too easy for a majority of family members to be taken over by some euphoric feeling that all their problems will disappear. At such moments often the needs and feelings of other members are not effectively taken into account. It is possible at the beginning of the change process for the natural cohesive strength of the family to become less than its usual level; indeed to create new solutions to old problems some loosening of the family's cohesion is necessary so that there is room in the rules and relationships for some movement and change. Therefore at this point the counsellor has to ensure the inclusion of everyone. The simplest way in which the counsellor can check on this is to ask everyone the 'What if' question, particularly in a way that builds on the replies of others.

Counsellor: What would you think about it, Sue, your mother and father visiting your brother?
Sue: That would be fine. It would be good to have some peace and quiet to myself at home.
Counsellor: And what about you, Andrew? We're talking about this and yet you're the most important one in it all.
Andrew: It would be OK but I think Dad would say 'No'. I don't think he'd want to come. I would also be nervous about Mum being critical about the state of the place, you know, about it not being up to her standards.
Counsellor: So you'd think your Dad would not be interested at all and your Mum too interested and you'd be on edge about both?
Andrew: Yeah.

In essence the counsellor is tracking hypothetical interaction and this in some senses can be seen as being an opportunity for the family mentally to rehearse some future action. This is important because it allows family members to deal with anticipated difficulties that may have prevented them from taking action previously. In the above dialogue it may be the first time that Andrew has expressed his belief about his mother's 'standards' and his emotional response to this. Clearly his views and feelings may have constituted a block against changing his interactions and this may have been the type of block that has remained unexpressed. By tracking the hypothetical interaction, the nature of a potential block can be revealed and the counsellor can decide whether to pursue this in this session or indicate that perhaps family members should consider it outside of the session.

As one of the counsellor's aims is to improve the family's ability to solve problems rather than just solve one problem, then an additional skill is needed in investigating the effects of a single action on everyone. In order to assist the family in building on their problem solving skills, the counsellor needs to **encourage interpersonal perception**. The purpose of this is to bring into open communication how one individual perceived the actions, beliefs and feelings of another person and attempt to ensure that those individuals can then discuss that perception meaningfully. To put it another way, each individual is encouraged to be more aware of their reflexive thought. 'If I do this X will think and do that and then I will do Y.' Here we are attempting to put into open discussion the 'X will think and do that' so that its accuracy can be tested.

> *Counsellor*: Andrew, what do you think your father would think if he heard you say that you don't think he's interested in visiting you?
>
> *Andrew*: I'm not sure. When I've told him he's not bothered about Mum, he just tells me I know nothing, discounting my view. So he should agree that he's not interested.
>
> *Sue*: You always say that but there's more to it than that.
>
> *Counsellor*: Sue has said something like that before. What do you think her view is, Andrew?
>
> *Andrew*: Well she thinks there's more to Dad than not bothering, you know, that he does care about me but I think he's got a funny way of showing he cares.
>
> *Counsellor*: So you know Sue sees your father as caring but even though she sees it that way, you don't feel what he does as caring?
>
> *Andrew*: That's right.
>
> *Counsellor*: What about you, Mrs Davies?
>
> *Mrs Davies*: Oh I don't know. He is a difficult man to talk to. I know I worry when I have to say difficult things to him.

Following these questions the counsellor always has a number of choices which essentially involve clarification and opening of communication. In the dialogue above the counsellor, for example, could have clarified Andrew's feelings about his father's behaviour. She does not do this. Instead she uses Sue's spontaneous contribution to encourage Andrew's interpersonal perception. Similarly, following Andrew's reply about Sue's perception the counsellor could have asked Andrew or Sue about their view of their differences of perception. As to why the counsellor pursued the line she did with the family is difficult to determine, and to some extent it is irrelevant for what essentially the counsellor is doing whatever path she follows is to allow the family to observe their own process. It is this mechanism of observing their own process and being able to communicate about it that develops the family's confidence in their own ability to 'heal' themselves. As they become aware of how their system operates they become more expert about themselves and this seems naturally to follow from the way the family interact. As families increase in their expertise about themselves, they are then able to follow through with their own problem solving strategies.

Box 7.1   Identifying problem solving strategies

1   Investigate previous solutions.
2   Investigate solutions that families have considered but not tried. Confront extremes.
3   Make embedded suggestions and effects.
4   Examine effects of a solution on everyone:
   (a)   by asking each person;
   (b)   by encouraging interpersonal perception.

Opening negotiations for adaptations for change

The process of identifying problem solving strategies may well be sufficient for some families in that their reflexive processes and interactive styles are flexible enough for them to take away those strategies identified and work on them. Some families, however, require a bit more of a push to do something different and in this situation the counsellor needs to be somewhat more forceful in her directions. It is not possible clearly to designate those families that need an extra degree of direction. In part it may come from the counsellor's estimation of the degree of rigidity within the family, and the extent to which the counsellor considers the family will communicate about the problem outside of the session. More importantly it will depend on the stated expectation the family had of counselling, for clearly those families which state they are looking for advice and guidance will be more amenable to direct suggestions from the counsellor than those with other expectations. Should the counsellor decide that there should be more direct negotiations for change it is worth while to remind the family of their expectations of counselling, either to point out how she intends to meet these expectations or to clarify the reason for her direction, given that it may not conform immediately to the family's stated expectation. It is also the case that different types of family problems require different amounts of direction at different times. Parenting issues do seem to respond to more open suggestions, as do some issues concerned with caring for a handicapped family member.

The first step in being more directive is to ask **questions that introduce a hypothesis**. Clinical hypotheses serve to provide tentative explanations that help orientate and organize the behaviour of the counsellor and they can provide a similar function to the self-healing behaviour of family members. The question format tends to convey the tentativeness that is important in systemic hypothesizing in that it does not imply certainty. It also serves the purpose of providing an explanatory background to the direct suggestions that may follow. The hypothesis should fit some element of the family's experience. If we follow our case example once again, the counsellor could be entertaining two hypotheses which explain some element of the family's difficulty:

1   That for some reason the family organize it so that Mrs Davies does not confront her husband without someone else being present. These reasons could be that Mr and Mrs Davies are fearful of what might happen if they were angry with each other alone. Or it may be that Andrew is worried what may happen if his parents are alone. This concern may have some historical origin.

2   That the family have not felt it safe for Andrew to 'leave home' without his frequent returns home and have organized it so he feels it necessary to be there.

Given these two hypotheses the counsellor could ask a series of questions each of which place the hypotheses before the family. Such questions might be:

1   'Andrew, who do you think is most fearful of an argument between themselves, your mother or father?'

2   'I have an idea, Mrs Davies, that it feels important to you to have someone present when you confront your husband. Why is Andrew safer than Sue?'

3   'Sue, it's beginning to look as if somehow it's arranged to have Andrew present when your mother and father have some business. Who do you think works hardest to make sure that arrangement occurs?'

4   'Mrs Davies, I'm thinking that Andrew is afraid of what might happen if you and your husband have an argument without him being there. How do you think he could be helped not to worry about that so much?'

5   'Andrew, it sometimes seems as if you have to be a 16-year-old at home rather than a 21-year-old with your own place. Who do you think prefers it if you are younger?'

6   'Sue, it seems to me sometimes that there is something in your family that wants everybody to be there. How do you think your mother and father will get on when you've left home or do you think Andrew will still be coming back to stay then?'

Of these questions, question 5 asks about Andrew's behaviour in terms of a certain developmental stage. Here somebody's behaviour is in a sense hypothesized as being that of a younger (or could be an older) person. This type of formulation can fit very well with most family's experience for, as in Andrew's case, the adults and Andrew himself have passed through the 16-year-old developmental stage and therefore they have intimate inter-active knowledge of it. Also the formulation of 'developmental' behaviour does imply changes occurring through time with development being the driving force and once again the process of movement is suggested. With all the questions each person's response should be surveyed in turn.

Once a hypothesis has been suggested and the counsellor finds that the family seem to work with it, then an increment can be made in terms of definite suggestion and this is done by a variant of the **'What would you say if I said . . .'** question. Here the counsellor outlines a possible clear suggestion with the tentative-ness maintained in the inquiry about a possible response rather than a statement which directly provokes a response. Hence if following such a question the person replied 'I wouldn't like it', the counsellor can follow up with a 'Well I won't say it then'. By this simple means the counsellor and family can maintain a negotiating style with each other without confrontation about the counsellor's suggestions developing. The counsellor in fact is looking for a suggestion that is going to be acceptable to the family. As with all elements of this aspect of the session, it is important that each member has their views and feelings checked out so that the process can go ahead smoothly. Let us return to the full dialogue in the Davies family session and we can observe how these two points come together.

Counsellor: I have an idea that it feels important to you to have someone present when you confront your husband. Why is Andrew safer than Sue?

Mrs Davies: Oh, it's not a question of safety. I'm not afraid of him. In many ways I'd rather not bother with him sometimes. I can do it without Andrew being there, its not important when he's not there but it becomes important when he is.

Counsellor: You mean it's important for you and for Andrew?

Mrs Davies: Well more for Andrew and perhaps even my husband but not for me so much.

Counsellor: So, I've got that a bit wrong. The people it's important for is first Andrew, then your husband, then you? I'm not sure what you make of that Andrew?

Andrew: I'm not sure. I just think he's not fair to her and she doesn't stand up for herself enough.

Counsellor: Right I understand your view but it seems as if your mother is saying that the argument between her and your father is more important for you and him than it is for her. Right, Mrs Davies? [*She nods.*] That must make you a bit stuck with it.

Mrs Davies: Yes that's right, I feel stuck because it is what the two of them expect. I'd rather leave things.

Counsellor: Well what would you say if I said that over the next couple of weeks when you have to raise important issues with your husband you should only do it when you and he are alone?

Mrs Davies: I could try it but I would be afraid they would argue anyway.

Counsellor: If they did, how might it start?

Mrs Davies: I'm not sure. They'd find something but at least it wouldn't be me starting things off.

Counsellor: That's what I was thinking. Andrew what would you say if your mother adopted that as a plan?

Andrew: I just don't like to think of her being walked over.

Counsellor: And who do you think is the best judge of that?

Andrew: I'm not sure.

Counsellor: Sue, I'm beginning to wonder whether or not Andrew respects your mother's perception about herself? How long do you think it's been like that?

Sue: Well as you can guess there's a difference between the men and women in our family.

Andrew: There you go again. Look, if Mum wants to do it that way then it's OK by me.

Counsellor: Well what would you say if I thought it a good idea to let
your mother get on with it with your father?
Andrew: Well I said I would.

In this dialogue we see that the counsellor's first hypothesis that
is put to Mrs Davies is erroneous but the way in which it was put
allows Mrs Davies to put her position more succinctly. Quite
correctly the counsellor does not dwell on the difference between
her own ideas and those of her client. The counsellor's ideas are
only flimsy constructions of infinite variability that are there to be
used by the family. Now that Mrs Davies has been able to
establish her position, the counsellor automatically takes this
position into account as she moves with the family to where the
changing of behaviour becomes a possibility. Although in the end
the suggestion from the counsellor may well have been exactly the
same regardless of whether Mrs Davies had agreed with her
hypothesis or not, the fact that there has been some clarification of
the position of individuals does augur well for the family following
through with the suggestion. We can see in this piece of dialogue
that the person least happy with the progress of matters is Andrew
and the counsellor, using another question, puts a hypothesis that
confronts this. However, the counsellor puts this question to
another family member so that if there is to be conflict in the
session it is more likely to occur between family members rather
than between the counsellor and family members.

The counsellor has now achieved the point where she can set
homework tasks. In doing this she should be clear what she expects
to happen and she should ensure that each person has a role
within the task, with each person being clear about their role. Of
course not everyone will have an active role in every task but it is
still important to specify that those who are 'inactive' should
carefully observe the behaviour of the active ones and help them
ensure they keep to the task specified.

Homework tasks in family counselling are not the same as
assignments given in behavioural counselling. Although some
family tasks may resemble and indeed be inspired by a behavioural
frame, they are dealt with differently. In the behavioural mode, the
professional is concerned with the specific construction of any task
and the specific outcome, in order that the behavioural analysis
may be refined and adjustment made to the contingencies. In
family counselling, the counsellor is similarly interested in the
outcome of a specific task in a behavioural sense but more
importantly she is interested in the 'task as information' to the
family. Whether the task 'succeeds' or 'fails', it will provide

important information about the family interaction and hence it maintains the momentum of therapy. A task should clearly place responsibility for problem solving within the client system. For the counsellor homework tasks can provide a variety of outcomes.

1   A simple straightforward solution – an intervention which may make a considerable difference and therefore represent a simple or straightforward solution. With the Davies family it could occur that following the task they return to the counsellor reporting a very successful outcome, so that Mrs Davies reports discussing matters with her husband in a way that proved helpful and realizes the boundaries she should now keep; as a result, she feels much more in control. Such events do occur, for often the act of talking to a counsellor is enough to mobilize the resources of the family to follow through with the simplest solutions. However, the counsellor is well advised not always to seek the quick solution in the first homework task. Any task, be it the first or the twenty-first, is just an opportunity to provide new information.

2   A recent event – this can then be tracked interactively whatever the outcome. The family will have attempted something different for themselves. Even with something that does not work, the interactions around this will provide information of a different order, either of how the family always manage to do something the same or how they did interact differently. Different and original material is therefore available for the counsellor to work with and this may indicate the particular interactive block that prevents an adaptive solution.

3   A 'new' opportunity – here the task offers an opportunity to clarify how the family organizes itself around something 'new'. Should a different or novel interaction occur as a consequence of a task, family members will have had their own experience of it such that exploration and clarification by the counsellor may provide considerably more 'newness' than was originally created by the task performance.

4   A means of understanding the 'distortion of communication' process. Some families will misunderstand the counsellor's task instructions and by openly comparing what the counsellor had anticipated happening with what did happen it is possible to identify one of the family's typical patterns of 'miscommunication', that is, the part in the interactive sequence which leads to particular outcomes rather than others.

5   An opportunity to assess how family members view their involvement in counselling. Occasionally a task will emerge in

one session and all family members agree that it is a useful thing to do and they will cooperate, but unfortunately at the next session the task does not seem to have been taken on board by some family members in a committed manner. When this occurs the counsellor should carefully return to individuals' expectations of counselling and, in particular, their expectations of the counsellor. This should be done in a careful 'unknowing' manner in order that the undoubtedly underlying conflict of views between family members can emerge.

The latter points in the list above will emerge as the counsellor monitors the task in a subsequent session; how this is achieved is described in the following chapter. Tasks require interaction in a situation where the currently held beliefs of family members block or distort elements of that interaction from occurring. Care must be taken in setting a task to ensure it provides a potential positive experience through directly confronting a prohibiting belief. Tasks therefore must lie within the range of what the family consider possible and this will only be determined by the process of the session itself.

To return to the setting of a task with the Davies family.

Counsellor: Look, it seems to me that the something to try, Mrs Davies, is to only discuss important issues with your husband when only you and he are present. A good thing to discuss is you both visiting Andrew. But also there is an important issue coming up soon because I would like you to discuss with him about him coming along to our next session. Andrew, it is important that you help by leaving your mother and father to get on with their discussion should it start with you there. It is important that you let your mother discuss these matters with him. You cannot take authority for that. Sue, I would like you to watch what happens and if Andrew seems as if he needs some help not to get involved, well you can help him with that.

Sue: Well, what if he does get involved? Should I stop him?

Counsellor: No, I don't think so. It seems to me that is up to your mother and father. Perhaps you should tell them so they can recognize it. Is that OK, Mrs Davies?

Mrs Davies: Yes I understand what you are suggesting – but I don't think it will get him here, and I don't think he'll want to visit Andrew.

Counsellor: I'm not sure but at least you have a go, regardless of the outcome we can see what happens. Who knows it may be something different.

We can now consider this to be the end of the session and the family can be left to get on themselves. In this case the counsellor is obviously expecting to have a further session and should determine with the family when the next appointment should occur. The optimal time gap between family counselling sessions is between two and three weeks. A time gap of less than two weeks often does not seem long enough, particularly for the family to try out new behaviours within the context of their daily routines of living. The family need to do something different and then see the consequences of that difference and this does take a little time. More than three weeks between appointments is too long, in that it becomes easier for old interactive patterns to establish themselves without the stimulus of a counselling session. Obviously this time gap applies just to the intensive period of counselling, for once some change has been established, it may well be that longer periods of time between sessions are more appropriate (see Chapter 8).

Box 7.2   Negotiations for adaptations to change

The counsellor should:

1   Introduce hypotheses.
2   Ask 'What would you say if . . .' questions.
3   Outline homework tasks.

8

Continuing and Closing

Flowers in spring
cuckoos in summer
moon in autumn
snow in winter
serene and cool

Dogen

It is helpful in travelling on any journey to know roughly where
one is, particularly if one intends to stop somewhere. In family
counselling, as part of the general process of assisting the family
reflect on themselves, the counsellor should check where the family
are in relation to their problem and their experience of
counselling. Although the issues discussed will have ranged far
and wide in the attempt to make changes that influence the family
system and its problem, the presenting problem – placed in its
interactional context – constitutes the ultimate reference point to
which all interventions and all assessments of those interventions
must be related. The family's experience of the problem and their
desire to make changes to remedy the situation define the **mandate**
that the family give to the counsellor. The mandate from the
family's perspective will define the boundary of the ongoing
therapeutic work that they consent to. The family's mandate
therefore sets a limit on the nature and extent of the interventions
and approach that the counsellor is 'permitted' to perform. With
the Davies family it will revolve around those problems that are
linked to the. presenting stress and control of diabetes. As Pinsof
(1983) notes, the problem – intervention link does not always have
to be direct and obvious but the process of sponsoring change
must always be conceptually tied to the problem and its
resolution. The connection between the presenting problem and
the intervention is the essence of the therapeutic mandate and all
counselling work should fall within this. By inviting the family
continually to review and reflect on the mandate that they bring,
the counsellor encourages a self-monitoring process which at some

point will lead on to the terminating process. Not only does the family need to monitor its own performance but the counsellor also needs to develop the means and techniques of reviewing her own behaviour in order that the direction of counselling is maintained. This chapter will therefore discuss the means by which the counsellor monitors her own as well as the family's progress before discussing how counselling is terminated. In order to provide in-counselling examples in this chapter, we will continue with the Davies family.

Box 8.1   Themes for dealing with the progress of counselling

1   Monitoring progress.
2   Dealing with blocks.
3   Maintaining direction.
4   Follow-up and termination.

Monitoring progress

Progress is monitored at the beginning of the session by the counsellor asking the family 'how are things going?'. Depending on the content of the reply, this is then followed up with clarifying questions: 'What happened that told you things were better/worse?', 'Were there any good/bad events last week?'. It is preferable not to inquire directly about the presenting problem *per se* but to ask about those interactions that have been established as being related to the presenting problem. 'Mrs Davies, last time we talked about how Andrew and Sue arguing caused some stress for you. How was that since we last met?' Once such information has been elicited the counsellor's task is to seek interactional reports of what has occurred between sessions in order to support family members' perceptions of progress. This method of checking on progress by tracking interaction is best demonstrated by the tasks that are necessary when the counsellor follows through on homework that was given in a previous session.

In the third session with our family one of the homework tasks obviously proved successful in that Mr Davies was present. The counsellor therefore began by welcoming him and generally getting to know him. The conversation continued:

Counsellor: Well, Mr Davies, to put you in the picture as to where we got to, we've been talking about the family difficulties, particularly the arguments, and how these might affect your wife's stress levels. We thought it was a good idea if we all met. I am wondering how did you discuss coming here?

Mrs Davies: Things seemed quieter at home. Andrew wasn't around so much and Sue seemed out more, so when we had a quiet moment I told Bryn [*Mr Davies*] about what happened last time and that I thought it helpful if he could come.

Counsellor: How did things go for you, Mr Davies?

Mr Davies: Well, things were definitely quieter. More time for me to think things through so we could deal with things calmly.

Counsellor: That's good. How did you find out your father was coming today, Andrew?

Andrew: Well he was ready when I arrived at home. I didn't know about it until then.

Mrs Davies: But you did ask me if I had done it though, didn't you? [*Andrew nods.*]

Counsellor: So what happened then?

Mrs Davies: Oh he asked me if I had mentioned it to Dad and I told him I was in charge of it.

Counsellor: That's good. Well done. What about you, Sue, when did you find out?

Sue: Mum told me this morning.

Counsellor: And did you know what happened between Andrew and your Mum?

Sue: No, but I was watching for it.

Andrew: I could tell you were watching for it.

Counsellor: Mr Davies, I don't know if you are aware but it seemed important that your wife ask you about coming along without the children being present.

Mr Davies: Oh I sort of knew that because my wife said. I was glad nobody else said anything.

Counsellor: Good. So what made it different for you, Mrs Davies? How do you think it worked?

Mrs Davies: Oh it was a case of picking the right time and with Andrew not around so much it made a difference.

Here the family, including the father, are clearly orientated to the themes around the task from the last session. If there had not been a homework task at this point, the counsellor would have needed to clarify the meaning of what occurred. Did everyone agree that this happened? What were each person's feelings about this? What were each person's perceptions of the others about this? This would then form the basis of monitoring with regard to the counsellor's mandate, namely did these things affect Mrs Davies's management of her stress? This may only be implicit in the discussion but it does need to be recognized as present. In this example, however, a homework task was given and the counsellor forgoes a discussion based on the preliminary statements of the family in order to focus on the task. This then serves as a link between one session and the other and gives the message to the family that when a task is set it will be followed through. The counsellor, however, only follows up on the existence of the task. She does not directly address herself to its specific content; to have been too focused on the exact content would be to treat the task in a behavioural manner rather than one from a family systems perspective.

The counsellor tracks the interaction in a way that the family can appreciate those elements of their behaviour that made a difference and those elements that were helpful in securing a positive outcome. The family's explanation for the change is also elaborated. The counsellor is looking for sequences in a new interactive chain that can be reinforced publicly. That the counsellor does this provides a model for the family also to positively reinforce that piece of behaviour. It also highlights an important marker of progress as, hopefully, when Mr and Mrs Davies can have a calm, quiet discussion, they can perceive it as a good sign, encourage it and so collaborate in a desired outcome.

If in this case the family had been referred with the problem of Andrew and Sue arguing the counsellor would have needed to follow through much more on the outcome of this. However, the family's mandate in this case involves the 'stress levels' of Mrs Davies and the counsellor needs respectfully to refer to this from time to time. This is simply achieved by the counsellor linking the above discussion to the presenting problem.

> *Counsellor*:   So did all of this have any effect on you, Mrs Davies?
> *Mrs Davies*:   At first I was worse. I was worrying, about finding· a good time. But when I did it was OK and that made it easier.
> *Counsellor*:   Good. Sometimes these things are more painful to go through but when you're on the other side it's much better.

Here a choice point arises. Should the counsellor go on to discuss the remaining aspect of the homework task or should she inquire whether aspects of Mr Davies's behaviour, such as 'taking a back seat', were stressful to his wife? Our counsellor decides on the former because of the way it is a metaphor for following through with rules for Mrs Davies and also because she believes the marital issue may emerge in the next task.

Box 8.2   Monitoring progress

The counsellor should:

1   Check with the family how matters are progressing.
2   Ensure homework tasks are followed through.
3   Track interactions of change within the family.
4   Check the family's explanation for change/no change.
5   Clarify the status of the presenting problem and its link to the issue under focus.

Dealing with blocks

Counsellor: I think the next issue was, Mr and Mrs Davies, you trying to find a way for you to visit Andrew and perhaps do something together like that.
Mrs Davies: We didn't get very far.
Counsellor: No?
Mrs Davies: Not at all really.
Counsellor: So what happened, Mr Davies?
Mr Davies: Well it just wasn't possible. It didn't happen.
Counsellor: So what did happen? [*Some silence.*] OK. Did either of you suggest you try?
Mrs Davies: I did, last Friday.
Counsellor: Last Friday, right, so what exactly did you say?
Mrs Davies: I said 'Let's go to visit Andrew this evening' and Bryn said 'No, I don't think we should. He might be out.' So we didn't go.
Counsellor: After he said that, did you say anything?
Mrs Davies: No, I just left it.
Counsellor: Is that how you saw it happen, Mr Davies?
Mr Davies: Yeah, I wanted to stay in and watch the television. Anyway I felt rather down. I didn't want to argue with Andrew.
Counsellor: Did you tell your wife that?
Mr Davies: No I didn't.
Counsellor: So would I be right, it didn't work out because it wasn't the best day, you felt down and didn't want to be upset.
Mr Davies: I suppose that's right.
Counsellor: What about you, Mrs Davies, why did you think it didn't work out?
Mrs Davies: Well my husband's attitude. I know he worries about himself sometimes, but he could show more interest in other things, things for us.
Mr Davies: I do but somehow you don't see, do you? [*A short period of silence.*]

Counsellor: Is this how it happens at home? That when you start to argue you become quiet, Mrs Davies?
Mrs Davies: I've found it best. I'm not very good at arguing back.
Mr Davies: But you will argue back about my things, but not about your things.
Counsellor: I'm sorry, I didn't understand that.
Mr Davies: Well, it's not right to say I'm not interested in things. I wanted to go to visit my sister. When I said let's go, she said 'No' and then gave lots of reasons for not wanting to go but when it's something she wants to do and I say 'No', she clams up. It's been the same since I was made redundant.

A failed task therefore is an excellent opportunity fully to appreciate the factors that are not allowing this family to deal effectively with the problems it confronts. These factors can operate at a variety of levels. In the above example we can identify the following:

1   The couple have not established a negotiating interactive sequence which they can use to move towards some solution. This is a straightforward lack of an interactive mechanism which is located very much in the here and now.

2   Mr Davies does seem to be indicating that during recent history (since his redundancy) dispute has arisen about how he and his wife should spend their time. The redundancy, as we have noted, is one of this family's major transitions and as such would have required some change in family functioning; such renegotiations do not seem to have occurred.

3   Mr Davies does not express his concerns to his wife about himself thus these feelings may not be allowed expression and acceptance within the relationship. This is at an emotional level which links to the couple's method of dealing with each other's feelings. This is a level which not only operates here and now but will also have been determined by the history of the couple as well as the personal history of Mr Davies.

4   Mrs Davies, it would seem, does not argue for what she wants but is willing to argue for what she does not want. Again this is at an emotional level and as with the above is related to the couple's ongoing system of dealing with each other and Mrs Davies's personal history.

Each of these 'blocks' can be hypothesized to be making a contribution to the Davies' failure to make progress with this issue. How then does the counsellor chose to prioritize which path to follow? This decision is made with reference to the FIRO model that was introduced in Chapter 2. When families experience life cycle transitions or major ongoing stressful events, they create new patterns of inclusion, control and intimacy. When challenged with a new situation there is an optimal sequence for creating new interactive patterns. First, the patterns of interconnectedness need to be determined so that the structure and boundary issues of inclusion are clear for everyone. Secondly, the marital bargaining over differences in role expectation – the control process, in which there is an agreed sharing of control interactions – is collaboratively established. Finally, any transition will require some changes in intimate interaction in which open self-disclosure and close personal exchange occurs. Therefore, following this model issues of inclusion have highest priority for successful resolution during family transitions because they are the bases on which successful adaptation in the control and intimacy area rest. Residual control issues then take priority over intimacy interactions. In the case of the Davies family we can see that the initial issue concerns where to place an effective boundary between Mr and Mrs Davies, as a couple, and Sue and Andrew as their children in early adulthood/late adolescence. To some extent progress has been made in this regard, in that the first homework task seemed to have produced some change. With the obstacles to the successful completion of the other task listed above, we see that hypotheses (3) and (4) are emotional intimacy issues whereas (2) is a control issue.

The FIRO model would therefore suggest that as inclusion has been dealt with, one should focus on hypothesis (2) as this involves the control issue of how Mr and Mrs Davies would deal with the problems around the redundancy. However, having decided to exclude hypotheses (3) and (4), and the FIRO model directing therapeutic activity to (2), this does neglect hypothesis (1) which covers a very basic interactive process within this family. Should we focus on the here and now process of hypothesis (1) or should we turn to a more recent historical process covered by hypothesis (2)? We can be helped in our decision by considering points made by Pinsof (1983) in his outline of an integrative model for family and individual therapy.

He discusses how, when a block is met, the most useful strategy in the search for a solution is to begin with the 'immediate, current interpersonal' solution and when this does not appear to work, then move towards more 'remote past intrapsychic' solutions. In our case we can consider that the homework task of Mr and Mrs Davies spending some time out together represents the most immediate current interpersonal strategy, and that unfortunately did not yield much in the way of measurable change. Therefore a task at the here-and-now end of the immediate–remote dimension has not worked, which then suggest a move along to 'less' here-and-now issues. As the negotiating interaction problem will be present in all time frames, it may indeed be beneficial to move the focus along and provide direction by discussing the 'control' issues between Mr and Mrs Davies as demonstrated in their pre-redundancy roles. Should this prove successful, then the issue of Mr and Mrs Davies sharing their feelings with each other will cease to be a block as they resolve the power problem. Equally, however, a focus on their expectations and collaboration about post-redundancy time may not take the change process far as the underlying problems of emotional intimacy prevent the negoti-ations for adaptations from taking place. Under these conditions the counsellor would then need to move the counselling focus more on to the themes of intimacy in the family. If such a direction should occur in this family's counselling, then it may well be that the counsellor finds herself discussing family of origin issues with both Mr and Mrs Davies. For a brief discussion and review of this approach, see O'Reilly and Street (1988).

The foregoing discussion should not suggest that there are rigid demarcations between inclusion, control and power issues; or that a counsellor only focuses at one time on here-and-now issues and at another time on there-and-then issues. Rigidity of this nature is certainly not a part of the counselling process. The frames of reference for the counsellor are only constructed to help make some moment-to-moment decisions in the welter of all the information present in the counselling session. The experienced counsellor will flexibly move through these reference frames and utilize them in different ways at different times, but there will, however, be general trends and the FIRO model and Pinsof's continuum of time frames provide good working rules of thumb for the counsellor.

Box 8.3   Dealing with blocks

1   Focus initially on the most simple solution.
2   Consider inclusion issues before control issues.
3   Consider control issues before emotional intimacy issues.
4   Move from here and now time frames to more distant time frames.

Maintaining direction

In monitoring progress the counsellor may consider that very little if any progress is being made. She may be faced with a situation where counselling is not going smoothly or not seeming to move towards a successful outcome. After initial hope the counsellor may feel inadequate to meet the family's needs and the issue of 'failure' will need to be confronted. Burnham (1986) lists various signs that indicate that the change process is not going well:

1   The counsellor working harder and harder without achieving any change at all.
2   The counsellor dreading particular family session (the phenomenon that Carpenter and Treacher (1989) refer to as 'Oh no, not the Smiths again'.)
3   Conducting sessions consisting of pleasant but aimless chat.
4   Arguing with a particular family member.
5   Devising increasingly elaborate plans for interventions with decreasing amounts of change.

Such signs indicate that the counselling system is stuck. If one holds on to a systemic view of this situation then clearly one cannot blame the counsellor or the family. The explanation for the impasse lies in the interaction between them and also in their respective interactions with the contexts in which they exist. Therefore when difficulties ensue in counselling there are three systems which need to be considered:

1   The family and its ecosystem.
2   The counsellor and the family.
3   The counsellor and her ecosystem.

The family and its ecosystem
When any client does not seem to respond to various types of psychological therapy, there is a tendency for those clients to be seen as lacking motivation. Bandler and Grinder (1975) recognize a process in language, which they term nominalization, where a verb is changed into a noun. This has the psychological effect of changing activity into an entity. Kingston (1984) notes that this has occurred with the concept of 'motivation' where it is now considered to be a thing that somehow resides within people. However if we change the noun back into the verb 'to motivate', we can recognize that individuals differ in the degree to which they are motivated to undertake a particular activity. If one changes the context, then those individuals may be motivated in different ways. Additionally, at any one time, one individual may be motivated to

undertake an activity that conflicts with another activity that he or she is motivated towards. This is known as ambivalence and is characterized by the presence of conflicting feelings and thoughts. Clearly, then, to be motivated in only one direction across all possible contexts is unreasonable. We are motivated to do things in one context and at one time but not necessarily others and the context in which we interact has a marked effect upon a person's willingness to take part in any activity, including activities dedicated to change. Motivation is not an all-or-nothing phenomenon, there are simply differences in the degrees of readiness to change and these will vary depending on context. Therefore to look at 'motivation' one has to consider the individual and family in context and there are four situations in terms of the family and its ecosystem that need consideration when family counselling may not be making significant progress.

The referral problem
As we saw in Chapter 3, the referrer is initially just as much a part of the system as family members and it may well be that the referrer is more of a customer than the family. With regard to motivation, we therefore may consider that the referrer is more motivated for family counselling than the family members. The initial caring system therefore needs to be considered very thoroughly in order to be clear about who is a customer and for what. Carr (1990) has catalogued the common mistakes that arise from not being clear about who the customer is, causing the engagement process to be distorted. Palazzoli et al. (1980b), in their paper entitled, 'The problem of the referring person', provide a typology of families enmeshed with referrers to the extent that therapy is sabotaged.

Example 8A

Mr and Mrs Vernon had two sons. The older boy, aged 8 years, throughout his life had had a number of hospital admissions for a heart condition. He was a rather sickly child and he required careful handling. The other boy, aged 6 years, was much more robust and from an early age, possibly in an attention seeking manner, would only eat certain foods – cereals, crisps, bread and butter. His weight and health were fine. The family doctor became concerned about this boy's eating when carrying out a general health check on family members. He referred the boy to a dietician who initially could not understand Mrs Vernon's lack of concern.

She discussed the matter with the doctor and they decided that Mrs Vernon was an 'anxious lady', that she had and continued to be 'over-focused' on the older boy and that Mr Vernon was 'not as involved as he might be'. The dietician and doctor made a referral for 'family counselling'. At the appointment Mr and Mrs Vernon explained how they were not concerned about their boy, they saw him as being fit and healthy and they felt they knew the diet he should be having. They were aware of the concern of other professionals and felt their reaction to be rather excessive. They reported the feeling of not being listened to. They believed that they were making slow progress with their son's diet and they felt his eating would improve gradually. No further sessions were offered.

When events like this occur, the counsellor should ensure that the referrer receives adequate and appropriate information on which to base his or her continued involvement with the family. It is desirable to prevent the referrer from becoming more of a customer for the family's counselling than the family themselves. In this sense a means needs to be found for indicating approval to the referrer for his or her action as well as approving of the family's action. The counsellor should directly address the referrer's concerns in an empathetic manner and indicate the value of the ceasing of further counselling action. In these circumstances family counsellors have to become adept at telephone calls and letter writing.

Is it the problem or is it the family?

As we have seen, families tend to react in typical ways to events that befall them and family histories tend to prescribe these reactions. Occasionally, however, a family has not been 'prepared' for particular events by their previous experience, hence the transitional crisis that follows the event can be of considerable proportions. In dealing with the event the family will be attempting to return to their traditional ways of coping and once a lessening of anxiety occurs and a sense of familiarity is achieved, the family will feel that they are back to 'normal'. Families arriving for counselling will need help in distinguishing between a solution to the problem *per se* and a 'solution' to their family functioning. Of course, at some level it is not useful to draw this line between 'problem' and 'family functioning' but it is apparent that following a transitional crisis families not only experience the transition as 'stress' but they can also experience their usual pattern of inter-action as stressful. There then is an increase in sensitivity to the family's typical functioning which may be experienced as dys-functional. Indeed every crisis brings with it the opportunity for new growth and families will vary in the extent to which they wish to move on from a crisis and deal with fundamental issues concerning their relationships. For some families the crisis will be finished when 'normal service' has been resumed. Other families will be only too willing to enter into an exploratory journey about themselves. We cannot ascertain how far each family will go, for as with other aspects of the 'motivation problem', this to a considerable extent will depend on contextual and historical factors well outside the counsellor's control.

Example 8B

Mr and Mrs Cooper had two children, Kathy, aged 4 years and Simon, aged 2 years. Simon had experienced difficulties in walking and recently had been diagnosed as having muscular dystrophy, a genetic wasting disease that led to handicap and early death. Following the news of this, Mrs Cooper had been very tearful, particularly with her best friend, her mother and professionals. Mr Cooper had just carried on 'as normal'. Mrs Cooper expressed her belief that her husband was bottling up his feelings about the diagnosis and she was very concerned about this. Mr Cooper did not easily discuss his feelings and thoughts with anybody but he felt that they would cope well. The social worker who supported families with this condition was concerned that there seemed to be a considerable amount of distance between the couple as exampled by their differing degrees of emotional expression. Mrs Cooper's mother also expressed this similar concern to the social worker in Mrs Cooper's presence with Mrs Cooper becoming even more tearful. The social worker discussed her worries with Mr and Mrs Cooper, who both readily agreed to attend for family counselling. At the counselling session it emerged that Mrs Cooper did tend to be much more emotionally expressive than her husband and that she was used to confiding in her friends and her mother. Mr Cooper thought it was better for the family if he did things his way and anyway he didn't know any different way. The couple were able to joke about their typical way of relating and both thought that under the stress of Simon's diagnosis their usual ways of coping had become extreme. As they wanted to do their best for their children they had come along for counselling as they were very willing to do whatever was necessary, but they did not see themselves becoming 'different people'. After the commencement of counselling the issues they discussed focused on the practical tasks they now faced and eventually this counselling task was taken over by the social worker.

Of course the male–female roles established by Mr and Mrs Cooper in the above example may come under further strain as their son's illness progresses. At the present time, however, the time is not right for these matters to be pursued vigorously – the family's mandate does not extend that far. The counsellor can ensure that family members have a good experience of counselling, for at another point in time they may consider that they do need help with this issue.

'We've got a problem', 'Oh no we haven't'
It can occur that one family member perceives there as being a problem and wishes to receive help, whereas another may either disagree that a problem exists or dispute the need for recruiting professional involvement. Of course, to be forewarned is to be forearmed, but in these circumstances should only one person turn up for the family interview, the counsellor, after establishing the nature of the problem, needs to establish with the person present the possible actions that can be taken. These actions may include convening family members from the extended family, organizing a session including professionals already involved with the family or communicating in a direct way with the person that has not attended. The aim of these actions is to change the frame of the way the matter would be discussed at home. To some extent this was done with the Davies family in the previous chapter. The approach of inviting others also serves to ensure that wider familial and social network influences would be dealt with in any subsequent session. Should this approach not prove successful, then the counsellor will need to take action which is then based on other aspects of his professional role, and this may well include 'Sorry we can't help this situation'. The counsellor should avoid at all cost pushing too hard for family counselling when all it achieves is an alliance with one family member against another.

Are other professionals helping?
Many families with difficulties have considerable contact with professional caring agencies and the caring system so constructed can become just as stuck as the family. Hardwick (1991) has listed the actions of professional networks which can hinder change. These actions include becoming overinvolved so that the family's autonomous action becomes impossible; backing off from a family

after much unsuccessful help so that the family is left floundering; different workers following different strategies, thereby cancelling each other out; providing so much help that an artificial world is created which protects the family from usual stresses; and scapegoating a family by insisting to the professional world that 'they aren't motivated'. Some particular types of family problem, which involve a number of agencies, can result in the agencies mirroring the interactions between family members between themselves. Reder and Kraemer (1980) have outlined how this process of replication occurs (see Example 8C). By approaching the referral process carefully the counsellor can pick up on the majority of these issues.

EXAMPLE 8C

Marcia Kingdom, aged 11, refused to attend school. She reported stomach ache and nausea each morning. Paediatric examination indicated no organic cause. Mrs Kingdom believed her daughter was frightened of school and with gentle care and understanding she could be slowly coaxed back. Mr Kingdom thought the 'muscular approach' was better than psychology. He believed she should be taken to school each day in a firm holding way. The parents argued about this and Marcia stayed at home. The professionals involved were in considerable contact with each other, the year tutor believed firmness was required, the pastoral care teacher felt that Marcia required understanding, the paediatrician instructed the parents that they 'shouldn't put up with this nonsense' and gave them an appointment in a month, 'just to make sure nothing is wrong with her', and the educational psychologist felt that Marcia needed some help in dealing with her own stress. It was noticeable that these divisions were also along gender lines with the males asking for structure and the females for understanding. The family were referred for counselling and no progress was made as the family constantly had differing contacts with professionals. It was only following a network meeting that progress was made.

The counsellor and the family
There are a number of fears which anyone who asks a professional for help can be expected to experience. Kingston (1984) lists these fears as being:

- Fear of being assessed as bad, mad or inadequate.
- Fear of being judged and condemned.

- Fear of finding out something terrible about oneself.
- Fear of being misunderstood (or worse being beyond under-standing).
- Fear of losing control over frightening aspects of one's life.
- Fear of private and intimate information not being kept confidential.

These fears will either be confirmed or allayed by the family's experience of the counsellor and unwittingly, even though he may believe he is allaying their fears, the counsellor's behaviour may unfortunately confirm them. The nature of the counsellor–client relationship can then itself become a barrier to progress. If we think about relationships in terms of repetitive patterns then it seems useful to remember that if we are not enabling a situation to change we are ensuring it is maintained. In these circumstances the one person whose behaviour we can change is ourself and this can be achieved via supervision.

Supervision
Every professional who has some 'hands-on' contact with clients requires the opportunity to receive supervision. As Hawkins and Shohet (1989) note, in order to maintain a 'good enough' approach to one's work one requires the strength of being held within and by a supervisory relationship. The same is true for counselling families as it is for every other branch of the counselling and therapeutic activity. This begs the question of what is 'good enough' supervision in this particular type of work. Unfortunately the development of supervisory styles and approaches within family therapy has sometimes led to confusion that a necessary element, if not a *sine qua non*, of family work involves a one-way screen, a team of observing colleagues and the technology of video taping. This is not so. Supervision in working with families is not high-tech in terms of equipment, but it certainly is a skilful process.

It is worth while briefly examining the history of families in treatment and the use of one-way screens. In the 1950s it became recognized in anthropological study that any trained participant observer will always, by virtue of being a human being, provide a biased view of the phenomenon being observed. Similar under-standing of the 'prejudices' of therapists and counsellors had also always been expressed. Such doubts about self report of therapists led therapy supervisors to prefer to watch their trainees interview families through a one-way screen or on video tape. This type of training supervision naturally led to the awareness that the supervisor was able to be more observant of the family interaction than the trainee and certainly more able to observe the trainee–family interaction. The use of the one-way screen therefore began as a training device (see Haley, 1976). It soon became apparent to those interested in an interactive, systemic approach that the observer/interviewer/family system had some properties which, if utilized, could be beneficial and thus approaches to family work developed in which the observers were seen as the 'therapists' and the interviewer was the 'conductor' (DeShazer, 1982). Strategies were designed which made use of the observer perspective (see Andersen, 1987). It is notable that these team approaches and techniques have developed in centres that specialize in the training of family therapists where the need for live supervision is paramount. As with co-therapy, there is no substantial research evidence that demonstrates the superiority of the hi-tech team approach over the lone professional meeting a family in an ordinary room (Gurman et al., 1985). Team 'supervision' approaches have, however, offered new perspectives on the nature of involvement between the client and counsellor but they do not define the field, and indeed they may well only be applicable to specific situations.

Team approaches tend to focus on the use of one-way screens (see Cade and Cornwell, 1985) and a number of authors have discussed the systemic properties of such a system (Speed et al., 1982; Burnham and Harris, 1985). Kingston and Smith (1983) have, however, discussed how a 'team' approach can be utilized with the colleague present in the room, thus discounting the need for the technical equipment.

The beginning family counsellor therefore needs to consider supervision in a general sense for her professional role as well as specifically for her family work. Problems will ensue for the counsellor if supervision is provided for either general professional work or specifically family work to the neglect of the other. Because of the nature of the interface between the professional's aims and duties and her activity as a family counsellor, it would undoubtedly be more efficient if the supervisor of one role has knowledge of the other. In some instances it will obviously be ideal if the same person supervises both roles. Within the terms of this text, however, it will be assumed that the counsellor has adequate professional supervision and has completed at least a basic training in working with families. Under these circumstances the counsellor will require the supervisor to address particular levels of the counselling process. These have been identified by Hawkins and Shohet (1989) as:

1 Reflection on the content of the counselling session. This is where the focus is on the actual phenomena of the therapy session, in order to enable the counsellor to pay appropriate attention to the clients and their statements. With the Davies family the counsellor wondered if she had only sketchily reflected Mr Davies's statements and that the content had focused more on his wife's comments.

2 Exploration of the strategies and interventions used by the counsellor. Here the focus is on the choice of interventions made by the counsellor in terms of what, when and why. Supervision at this level aims at increasing the counsellor's choices and skills in intervention. The supervisor and counsellor in discussing the Davies family concentrated on the counsellor's decision to invite only the couple to the forthcoming session.

3 Exploration of the counselling process and the relationships created by it. The main aim here is for the counsellor to develop greater awareness and understanding of the dynamics of the relationship between herself and the family. It is the element of supervision when the interaction between counsellor and family is considered very closely. As such the approach the supervisor takes may be similar to the general counselling approach outlined here. An example of this supervision issue is with the Davies family in the previous chapter where the counsellor wondered whether her interactions with Sue, Mrs Davies's daughter, had been dictated by the other family members as Sue was involved in a helpful way, but the counsellor felt that there was little contact between herself and Sue. The supervisor and counsellor then began to consider who might Sue be in close contact with in the family and how the nature of that relationship could be brought into the sessions. In this general area the supervisor and counsellor should give careful thought to whether the counsellor is by her activity simply replicating a particular family role. The familiarity the family have with particular interactions tends to create an automatic position as 'family member' that an unwary counsellor could easily fill.

The above issues all involve a concentration on the counselling session itself and this can be achieved by the supervisor and counsellor discussing the session following the counsellor's report or via video or audio tape of a past session or via live supervision. The remaining issues of supervision identified by Hawkins and Shohet involve concentrating on the counselling process as it is reflected in the supervision process.

4   Focus on the counsellor's feelings and thoughts. Here the supervisor concentrates on whatever is being carried by the counsellor, both consciously and unconsciously. The counsellor seeing the Davies family felt it difficult dealing with Mrs Davies's occasional diffidence as it reminded her of an aunt of hers.

5   Focus on the supervisor's feelings and thoughts. It is necessary for the supervisor to tune in to him or herself during supervision in order to explore how evoked feelings, thoughts and actions in supervision may have an implication for the process in counselling. The supervisor in the Davies case kept on having the image of a 'higgledy-piggledy' house. The counsellor and supervisor took this image and used it to develop some thoughts about how the family might organize their home life.

6   Focus on the here-and-now process as a mirror or parallel of the there-and-then process. Here the supervisor focuses on the relationship in the supervision session in order to explore how it may interactively parallel the interactions and dynamics of the therapy session. For example, with the Andrews family (see Chapter 4) the supervisor noted how the counsellor merely raised issues and waited for the supervisor himself to provide some direction, and when this was pointed out, the counsellor became aware that a similar interaction had occurred in the session with everyone raising issues and waiting for him, the counsellor, to 'do something'. This then allowed the counsellor to recognize the very strong invitation from the family to be an 'expert' for them but each member had an expectation of a different 'expert' with the consequence that the counsellor tended to be triangulated in each dyad's conflict (mother–son, mother–daughter-in-law, husband–wife). As the interactions between the counsellor and supervisor can be discussed beneficially, it is also possible that these interactions could also have negative effects on the counsellor's work. Carpenter and Treacher (1989) have discussed these effects and outlined how 'stuck' counsellor–supervisor systems can be mobilized.

These levels of supervision focus on different aspects: the first is 'case-centred', the second and fourth are 'counsellor-centred', while the fifth is 'supervisor-centred'. The 'interactive-centred' approach is contained within the third and sixth levels and these are the levels that counsellors from a family systems background will obviously be more interested in. Hawkins and Shobet note that if a supervisor focuses exclusively on the interactive approach then there are fewer dangers of poor direction than with supervision that concentrates on other approaches. The only drawback from such exclusivity is that a great deal of useful information is ignored. Therefore the counsellor in choosing a supervisor needs to ensure that the supervisor can range across all approaches while being adept at discussing matters interactively.

The counsellor and her ecosystem

The counsellor's ecosystem involves both her private life as well as her professional life. How the counsellor functions within her personal family system will have repercussions on her functioning in her professional life. The need for counselling and therapy for counsellors and therapists and the need for other self-care activities is well known. These issues will not be dealt with further here save to say that every counsellor needs to take responsibility for her own well-being; it is an essential element of a professional commitment in this work.

Away from home life every counsellor is embedded in a system of relationships to other professionals. Most relationships are collaborative within the guidelines of set objectives and organized within a formal structure which can be termed an agency. The agency itself will have a variety of interconnections through its employees' professional liaisons with other workers. Even the lone private counsellor will have an ecosystem of professional relationships but they will not be as closely collaborative or organized as the employed professional and hence the liaison function with other workers may be at a minimum.

In a manner similar to families and other human systems, agencies develop ideologies to help explain the phenomena they meet so that they can then communicate with the outside world. As with families, the ideology is necessary so that ongoing and future events can be related to in predictable ways. Within agencies, however, the ideology is maintained via the objectives, the formal hierarchy and the general professional goals of the employees. Each agency ideology will particularly address the nature of the problems that it was constructed to deal with. The ideology will define how the problems arise, how human action related to the problems is produced, how human development proceeds and how the problems diminish. Thus a medical agency may see problems arising from biological dysfunction with human action being produced biologically along the physiologically defined developmental stages and the problems being cured via pharmacological means. Social welfare agencies, agencies involved with educational establishments, agencies composed of only one professional group etc., will have very different ideologies. The agency ideology also serves to specify the nature of the interaction between the change agent and the client. It will define the purpose of the interaction, outline its content and specify where the focus of control for change lies; this definition will also cover the way clients who disagree are viewed. Returning to our medical agency example, the purpose of change agent interaction is to provide a cure. This is done by noting symptoms and making a diagnosis and the change agent is perceived as being the person in control of the treatment that is offered, that is, the doctor, and should a client disagree, that client is seen as being a 'non-compliant patient'. Obviously this example is rather stereotyped but it does make the point about the pervasiveness of the ideologies of the agencies within which we work. There are unfortunately too few agencies that have an ideology embracing the family system view (see Street and Reimers, 1993).

Although agencies have ideologies that are in contrast to a family system perspective, it is possible for individuals and groups of individuals to have their practice informed by a systemic view. Most professionals who employ family counselling and its techniques do so from a position of being in an agency which permits and condones such practice but which does not embrace the perspective in terms of its organizational and administrative goals and structures. (For a discussion of a systemic approach to the administration of a treatment agency see Todd (1984); and for a discussion of private practice see Dammann (1984).) It is in the interface between the tasks faced by the professionals in their agency role and the tasks of family counselling that most of the problems in maintaining a direction emerge. As with the family's mandate for counselling that was referred to earlier in the chapter, it can also be considered that there is a mandate between the professional and her organization that she will apply her professional skills to meet the stated objectives of the agency. If we take the example in this chapter of the Davies' family counsellor, she is employed by a health agency to provide family support to patients with diabetic problems; sometimes that role will involve active family counselling as with the Davies but at other times it will involve educational work, practice advice, liaison on behalf of patients etc. Her family counselling activity is permitted as long as it is within the boundary of providing 'family support' for Mrs Davies. Under these circumstances we would expect the counsellor to be very familiar with particular problems, that is, health problems and coping with diabetes. In some agencies the workers will be very familiar with particular stages of the life cycle, for example, child guidance clinics etc. Although the counsellor has a generic view of the family life cycle and although her skills theoretically are applicable to any family with any type of problems, her skills are tied to the mandate given her by her agency, which in turn is linked to the presenting problem and the counselling mandate. In our example it could have been that Mrs Davies first presented in a different way and thus a different context would have been constructed. In talking about her problems with her doctor, Mrs Davies may have told the story solely and directly in terms of the difficulty her husband was having with his redundancy; the doctor may have discussed this with the family support worker who, holding firmly on to her agency's mandate, may have considered that the couple were more appropriately referred elsewhere. The counsellor's agency role hence dictates the task of finding a way of helping Mrs Davies ensure her husband receives help. Obviously, if the counsellor in this case spent time offering direct help to all the unemployed husbands of patients with a diabetic condition, she would have little time to undertake her other duties.

This discussion about the kinds of agency mandate is particularly relevant for one major problem with progress, and that is the issue of trying to do too much. There is no agency that employs professional staff where the ethic is 'you must solve every problem' – such an agency and such a standard for work does not exist! A common occurrence amongst counsellors and therapists of every persuasion, however, is the feeling that 'my skills are not extensive enough – if only I were better, I could really help this family'. Whenever counsellors feel inadequate they should first remind themselves of their agency's mandate and then remind themselves that the family take responsibility for themselves. Nearly all problems of trying too hard or to do too much stem from the counsellor attempting to reach the 'perfect' standard of the agency's mandate. When this occurs the general professional role of the counsellor becomes lost as the counsellor tries to enhance a family system's functioning that may not be capable of being enhanced. The fantasy of being an ideal counsellor conflicts with the practical day-to-day tasks of the counsellor in her professional role and in order to be able to prevent this the counsellor needs the ability to say she has gone as far as she can. This can be demonstrated with what transpired with the Davies family. The counsellor spent some sessions focusing on Mr and Mrs Davies' relationship without their children but unfortunately little progress seemed to be being made. The counsellor begins with a general monitoring question.

Counsellor: How do you think we are doing, Mr Davies?

Mr Davies: Things are the same.

Counsellor: Do you think things can change, sometimes I wonder how far we are getting.

Mr Davies: Why should things change? If my wife could be calmer we wouldn't be here. We can't change the fact I haven't got a job

Counsellor: What about you, Mrs Davies?

Mrs Davies: No we can't change some things. I know that. It would be better if things were better. I don't think it's about me being calmer – I am calmer now, but perhaps at the end of the day we have to deal with what we've got and be content with that.

Counsellor: Do you mean for both you and your husband?

Mrs Davies: Yes, that is both of us.

Mr Davies: I agree with that.

Counsellor: You both seem to be saying we have to accept things we can't change.

How would we evaluate such a situation? Some things may not have 'shifted' very much. There is still some disagreement. Perhaps the couple's expectations are too different. Mrs Davies says 'I am calmer' – this self report could qualify as evidence of a 'success', namely reducing Mrs Davies's stress level. But her husband disagrees. Who can truly say what all these statements add up to. It is clear that offering 'more of the same' in terms of family counselling is not likely to produce any further change. The counsellor can, however, be satisfied that she attempted to help the family with her skills to the limit of her agency mandate and providing that she closes the current counselling context in a professional manner then she can do no more. There are many events and situations in life which we would like to perceive as problems for which solutions can be found, but in the end they are simply events and situations that are difficult to deal with. Not every problem finds a solution and sometimes we just need to find coping strategies. This discussion has centred on an examination of the limitations placed on counsellors by their agency ideology. However, it may well be that a counsellor, on feeling stuck with a particular family, may find that professional supervision about this family and the agency could generate new ideas which can enhance the tasks of counselling.

Dealing with the unchangeable

Our counsellor with the Davies family continues with her monitoring of their progress.

Counsellor: So if you feel that you are still not involved with each other as you would like. How are you going to cope with that?

Mrs Davies: Perhaps I need to do some things on my own. He could do his own things his way but I don't have to.

Counsellor: No, I guess not. What about you, Mr Davies – if you still think your wife is not calm enough but that it can't change, how are you going to cope with that?

Mr Davies: I think I have for a while – in my own way. It's just that my wife doesn't like that way and I have no other way of doing it so I'll just carry on as before.

Counsellor: You both seem sad and disappointed about it.

Mr Davies: Yes, there's a lot to be sad about and I am disappointed that things are not different. But our life is as it is. My wife has an illness and I don't have a job.

Counsellor: And I guess nobody's to blame for those things?

Mrs Davies: Well yes, in a way. Perhaps the person who put Bryn out of work. But we can't change what we've got. We just have to live with it.

This is a task of counselling, allowing individuals and families to come to an acceptance of the cards that life has dealt them. Of course there are some individuals in Mr Davies's situation who will see redundancy as being a challenge to himself, a way to find a new meaning of himself. It is possible to discover the vast extent of human growth in and through adversity. This discovery will undoubtedly involve touching on the nature of spirituality for any particular person. This is possible through counselling, therapy and other techniques but it does not appear to be the case for Mr and Mrs Davies and this needs to be recognized by the counsellor. In fact, we find Mrs Davies touching on what is a spiritual theme for herself, namely that one deals with adversity by putting aside negative feelings towards self and others and then accepts it in the best possible way. That, of course, is not the only spiritual comment that one could have about what to do in the face of this situation, and counselling could obviously offer a discussion of this, but it is not the case for Mrs Davies at least and we need to respect her view and deal with her and her family accordingly.

This discussion has much relevance to the counselling of families who are dealing with 'problems' that are unsolvable – the grand-mother who has Alzheimer's disease, the child chronically handicapped, the father dying of cancer. As counsellors we can address emotional and psychological difficulties that are associated with these events and we can help families solve 'problems', increase their 'awareness' and give people a positive attitude to dealing with life, but ultimately we cannot change the unchange-able. Even though the 'unchangeable' is merely a notion in somebody's mind, ultimately families will always define what is unchangeable for them and we, as counsellors, have to give that view the respect it deserves.

Follow-up appointments and termination

As a family report progress, a greater time gap between appointments may become appropriate. Depending on specific contexts, different counsellors deal with this issue differently. Some use the mechanism of an ever-increasing timespan between sessions, finally nominating the next one as being the 'last one'. Others may agree in the contract they set out with the family beforehand that when the counselling sessions are deemed to have finished then there will be a follow-up appointment some months later. Whatever strategy is adopted it is of course preferable that the agreement fits in with the wishes of the family. Research has indicated (Wolberg, 1980) that planned follow-up at a three-month distance can have productive therapeutic impact, particularly if it is presented as an integral part of the process during the initial meeting. Therefore it is beneficial for counsellors to indicate the value of such a follow-up. Treacher (1989) has identified five categories of follow-up:

1 **The safety net**: some families may feel their change processes to have only been minimal or transient but the counsellor considers that the family would be helped more to lauch themselves back into their own life without reliance on ongoing sessions by offering follow-up which offers to provide a safety net should matters not progress well.

2 **The routine check**: this is a more matter-of-fact follow-up along the lines of 'let's meet again in six months' time just to check out what is happening'.

3 **The research follow-up**: counsellors and agencies do need to evaluate their effectiveness and a variety of formal and informal techniques exist for this. Treacher (1989) makes the point that such contact should be planned in order to be beneficial to the family.

4 **Telephone follow-up**: a brief telephone call to a family can serve instead of an interview. It is a useful strategy when counselling has gone well and when there may not be the need for a full family session. Occasionally it can also be used where a family is anxious not to terminate 'finally' but needs to be aware of the availability of the counsellor.

5 **Failure follow-ups**: This is the follow-up where the counsellor finds some way of contacting the family that failed to continue

with counselling. This may be by inquiry letter, telephone call or request to a referring agent. Counsellors should give considerable thought to their practice with this type of follow-up as the only message the family should receive is one about the continued availability of the counsellor.

The nature of the follow-up will largely depend on the client group. For example, families dealing with chronic illness may benefit from a number of follow-ups over considerable periods of time, whereas families with problems that relate specifically to transitional crises will be helped more by the 'just once' follow-up. In the case of the Davies family, it would seem appropriate to arrange one follow-up appointment, particularly to review the progress of Mrs Davies's stress and diabetic control.

Termination

As with the term 'motivation', similar problems of prescribing particular expectations emerge when one uses the concept of termination. Termination implies that something is being ended and hence whatever was happening before will cease to happen after. In terms of the notion of change being presented here, the difference between before and after is that the family no longer meet the counsellor but this does not mean that the interactive change process embarked on will also cease. Indeed, as Combrinck-Graham (1981) notes, the end-point of family work is difficult to define because the notion of the family life cycle cuts across the idea that a family is ever in a 'correct' state; it is in continual movement and the notion of a set of circumstances which can be identified as a 'cure' is impossible to sustain. Also, as Heath (1985) comments, if one adopts a model of respecting clients to monitor their own health and need for ongoing help, then families may choose an overall entry–exit–entry–exit sequence of contact with their counsellor. If this should happen, provided the family are not just repeating the same process over and over, one may consider that the idea of a termination could be replaced with the notion of 'terminations', with all that that implies. Indeed, as the process of monitoring is a core feature of the session-to-session process, the questions posed from the monitoring position continually present to the family a potential discussion about ceasing the ongoing contact. The family is responsible for terminating counselling and by accurately listening during the monitoring process, the counsellor will be able to open the discussion into one where ceasing contact is a theme. In doing this a particular set of questions follows. These questions will be presented together with the replies given by the Davies family.

1   What happened to the problem?

> *Counsellor*: Where are we with the original problem? Mrs Davies, your stress levels and the things happening in the family that weren't helping that?
>
> *Mrs Davies*: I feel better about how things are with my son and daughter and Andrew himself seems to set himself up well. I'm not sure how we're getting on, me and my husband. Perhaps I do feel less stressed but my diabetes hasn't improved a great deal – but the doctor is checking on it.

2   How do the family explain this occurrence?

> *Counsellor*: Why do you think these things have happened like this?
>
> *Mrs Davies*: Well I think we became clear about Andrew's visiting. It was pleasing that we made the changes towards him, it helped him and us. But in terms of me and my husband, I'm not sure if we've changed much between us. We seem to be expecting different things from this situation and I now understand that.

3   What was the role of everybody in this change?

> *Counsellor*: How do you feel each person contributed?
>
> *Mrs Davies*: Well I do think we all understood what we were trying to do, even my daughter, and it just worked
>
> *Counsellor*: Is that how you saw it, Mr Davies?
>
> *Mr Davies*: Yes, we soon found a different way of dealing with it.
>
> *Counsellor*: And what about the two of you and how you negotiate things?
>
> *Mr Davies*: Well, as my wife says, we have different ideas about how to deal with me around so much. Just different that's all and we have to accept that.
>
> *Mrs Davies*: I would have liked more things to have happened but well, my husband does what he does and I suppose it's OK. It is not going to ruin us.

4   If a similar problem emerged again, what would the family do?

> *Counsellor*: So, if these problems emerge again – how will you deal with that?
>
> *Mr Davies*: We'd have to make sure we're clear about the rules that apply for us and if we're not then work them out.
>
> *Counsellor*: I suppose as Sue moves away these types of issues could arise again.

The counsellor here has drawn the family's attention to the next predictable transition in the life cycle and in doing so highlighted the next possible set of problems the family has to solve. This may help them prepare for what is to come.

5 Why do the family think it happened in the first place? This could lead to discussion which contrasts the family's new beliefs with their old ideology.

Counsellor: Looking back, how do you think this problem started?
Mr Davies: I don't think we were clear about how to help Andrew leave home properly and well I just sat back and let my wife get on with it.
Mrs Davies: Yes that's right, but then it becomes difficult to know when to say 'enough is enough'. We just didn't draw a line at the right time.
Counsellor: That seems different from when we first met.

6 Check the family's desire for ceasing:

Counsellor: What about more appointments?
Mrs Davies: Do you think we need to come again? Things do seem better.
Counsellor: I'm happy if you're happy. What do you think of that, Mr Davies?
Mr Davies: It's fine by me.
Counsellor: It happens like this often doesn't it, Mrs Davies? You make some comment and I then try to get Mr Davies involved?
Mrs Davies: Yes but you can't change the habit of a lifetime. [*All laugh.*]
Counsellor: No I don't suppose you can. I think it's fine you feel there is no reason to come again.

The counsellor continues to take the opportunity to comment on interaction in the room.

7 What would be a sign that the family needed more counselling?

Counsellor: How would you know if you needed to come back to see me?
Mrs Davies: Oh I suppose if I were stressed again.
Counsellor: How would you know that?
Mrs Davies: I suppose if I was worrying about the family again.
Counsellor: What about you, Mr Davies?
Mr Davies: As my wife says, if she starts to worry more, I think then.
Counsellor: What about what happens to you?
Mr Davies: Oh I'll just carry on in my own way. It's if my wife needs the help.
Counsellor: Fine, but I suppose we have no way of knowing how things will develop for you as time goes on.

As the counsellor goes through this relatively routine bit of questioning we can see that she supports their decision about termination and she reinforces their view about this. She still takes the opportunity to comment on the interactive pattern so that the family are reminded of their problem solving interaction which may or may not require a counsellor. The counsellor also seeks to clarify the explanations the family have to account for the gains made; for some families this will be a particularly important process as it helps them to verbalize to themselves and each other the interactive mechanisms by which they came to make changes. Some families will need help in this way to maintain a 'public' awareness of how they go about dealing with their difficulties. As these changes are outlined by the family, the counsellor is then able to reinforce the differences that have been made. Throughout, the counsellor is continually orientated towards the future so that the seed is sown about the possibility of problems in time to come; problems that can be faced without trepidation and without the thought that 'failure' has occurred.

Box 8.4   Termination

The counsellor should:

1   Support the family decision about termination.
2   Clarify the reason for gains made and link to the family's original 'theory' of the problem and expectations of counselling.
3   Reinforce changes made.
4   Be future-orientated (refer to future life cycle tasks).
5   Indicate the continued availability of counselling.

Finally, the counsellor deals with matters in such a manner that her door is always open and future work may indeed be necessary. There is a sense in which the counsellor provides the family with a 'ghost' of herself, an image of her person and activity that can be used to remind the family of positive ways of confronting their problems. The counsellor is now within the family's collective memory, she has become part of their story and in her struggle to become an effective counsellor they have become part of hers. The story goes on for everyone and the interactions of the counselling context may be required again.

9

Back to 'One'

There is no first cause. There is a circular cause, in which the
beginning, which does not exist, meets the end, which is
impossible.

Maurice Maeterlinck

A basic method used in the teaching of meditation focuses on
counting the breath. On reaching 'Ten' the meditator goes back to
'One'; should the mind become distracted, losing the count, then
once again 'One' is returned to. Therefore there is no 'success' or
'failure' for whatever happens 'back to One' occurs. The meditator
becomes skilful on going back to 'One' and the process in a single
act focuses the mind on the moment. All counsellors and therapists
instinctively develop a process of 'back to One' when they need to
return to a beginning. The best way to indentify this is to ask the
question, 'When I feel stuck in a session and am not sure what I
want to do, what do I do?'. The answer should reveal where 'One'
is for you; it should reveal the skill you use that forms the basis of
your response to the situation. In the development of that personal
response each of us needs to be informed about the 'One' to 'Ten'
of family counselling. It is our 'scientific' activity, our conceptual
and perceptual endeavours which attempt to provide that
information in a general way for us. To do this we need to
consider the 'research' in this field and the skills necessary to
produce effective counsellors.

Science and research

In the introductory chapter the systems perspective on natural
phenomena was outlined. This, as Goldberg and David (1991) point
out, forms the characteristics of the 'new' science. This model of
inquiry has critiqued the basis on which 'old' science attempts to
know and understand the world. The 'old' view holds that cause
and effect can be understood, it being possible to make observations
which are objective and independent, with those observations being

understood as outlining the 'truth'. The critique of the traditional approach has called into question the nature of research inquiry into counselling and providing therapy for families. The two principle themes raised by this criticism have been those of objectivity and causality. The systems view challenges the traditional cause and effect model, with circular causality implying no distinction between 'independent' ('cause') and 'dependent' ('effect') variables. Thinking systematically does not merely require us to investigate a larger unit of analysis but also to investigate how the elements that make up the unit are connected and patterned. It invites us to investigate the interdependence of all phenomena. It is also argued (Auerswald, 1987) that the researcher is not able to be objective and the measures, methods and constructs used are nothing other than the researcher's way of 'punctuating' phenomena. Goldberg and David (1991) have argued, however, that in a general and specific sense the new systemic thinking should incorporate and be incorporated by the more traditional scientific endeavours. Gurman (1983) illustrates this in the numerous ways 'traditional psychotherapeutic research designs implicitly involve systemic concepts of context, connectedness and interdependence'. For example:

1   The study of the interactive effects of patient, therapist treatment and setting variables.
2   The use of multidimensional change measures.
3   The use of multiple vantage points for assessing change.
4   The use of repeated measures to assess both levels and patterns of change over time.

Thus it is not appropriate to discard the 'old' simply because the 'new' has appeared, particularly as the 'new epistemology' has not effectively translated its approach into practical research projects. In this respect, however, it should be noted that the more recent development of audit methods within medical and allied activities involves an approach that is essentially systemic (see Chase and Holmes, 1990).

So what does scientific endeavour tell us about the progress in this field? In the last major research review on marital and family therapy Gurman and his colleagues (Gurman et al., 1985) state that it has now been 'established convincingly that in general, the practice of family and marital therapy leads to positive outcomes'. Amongst their general conclusions, they point out that:

•   The developmental level of the identified patient (for example, child/adolescent/adult) does not affect treatment outcomes significantly.

- Positive results typically occur in treatments of short duration, that is one to twenty sessions.
- Deterioration of individuals and relationships sometimes does occur.
- A style of providing little structure in early treatment sessions and confronting highly affective material may be reliably associated with observed deterioration compared with a style of stimulating interaction and giving support.
- A reasonable mastery of technical skills may be sufficient for preventing worsening or for maintaining pre-treatment family functioning but more refined relationship skills seem necessary to yield genuinely positive outcomes.

In other words, it works when used skilfully, but how does it work?

Greenberg (1991) has argued that the approach to psychotherapy research typified by most of the work reviewed by Gurman and his colleagues is in fact defensive in that it merely attempts to justify the existence of the therapeutic approach rather than attempt to discover how it works and what leads to change. If this could be done, then one could go on to specify the necessary skills to produce change. Greenberg presents a process-analytic approach to psychotherapy research based on what he terms the world of 'Understanding'. This approach is similar to the views outlined in this book, in which the importance of meaning and the testing out of that meaning is stressed. Greenberg suggests that what is required is a study of the similarities of performance and experience of individuals involved in similar therapeutic situations. Hence 'change performances in specific behavioural contexts which are similar . . . are studied to isolate common features and process'. His fundamental assumption is that in specified therapy and counselling contexts, behaviour and experience are lawfully explainable and valid specific models or micro-theory can be developed to help explain therapeutic change processes. Clearly in our designated field of family work we do not seem to have begun to elucidate possible explainable laws, and as Pinsof (1981) has remarked, family therapy is not informed by a micro-theory of its processes. In our field we have not as yet outlined the basic foundation skills necessary for family systems change.

Skills analysis

When it comes to discussing skills, theories of family therapy and counselling have tended to be expressed in terms at a high level of generality, hence they do not provide operational definitions of skills which could aid the construction of notions of counsellor performance which would be available to study. Unfortunately, there is a general lack of refined models for analysing skills so that they can then be reconstructed through the training process (see Street, 1988). Cleghorn and Levin (1973) provide a categorization system based on perceptual, conceptual and executive skills. Developing on this tripartite division, Tomm and Wright (1979) have operationalized a number of skills which are based on the process element of counselling and therapy sessions defined within terms of engagement, problem identification, change facilitation and termination. The latter analysis could be utilized to categorize the skills that are outlined in the body of this book. However, this analysis is based on the time process in that it outlines how one begins, moves through the middle and then to the end. It does not deal with the processes of encounter between counsellor and client and it does not deal with foundation skills that are necessary in order that the more complex skills sufficient to produce change may be produced. This introduces the notion that the skills of counselling and therapy should be considered in terms of their hierarchical arrangement, in that skills are necessary at one level in order that skill production at the next level is rendered possible. Following the ideas expressed throughout this work, it would appear that a three-level model of skills can be constructed and this is outlined in Table 9.1.

Table 9.1 *Skills model*

Level	Basic attitude	Skill
1	Respect	Structuring
		Reflection of feeling
		Reflection of interaction
2	Inquiry	Reflexive questioning
		Clarifying
		Opening communication
3	Action	Breaking maladaptive patterns
		Identifying problem solving strategies
		Negotiating for adaptation to change
		Providing information
		Terminating

The model is presented in a way that specifies a basic human attitude, something that is common to us all, and links that attitude to specific skills which have been described and demonstrated here. At the foundation level is 'respect'. This could also be termed acceptance, warmth, regard, love. It is the attitude of valuing others for what they are, trusting what they are and what they can become, as well as trusting that they have respect for us. Without this basic relational attitude towards other people we cannot hope to be invited into the private world of their successes and failures to assist them with their personal struggles.

At the next level we have the attitude of inquiry. Humans are conscious animals who seek to understand the world through their thinking. The process of being intrigued, curious, fascinated by the world, leads to a wish to relate to it in a way that its workings are revealed to us. However we term it, the process of inquiry always opens up new vistas and perspectives for our understanding; so too with families as with individuals. Inquiry is linked hierarchically to the preceding attitude for before curiosity there must come respect. As family counsellors, when we join and collaborate with families we respect, then the path of inquiry is made much easier.

The final level is the 'doing' part of human activity. Action for humans brings into play their ability to use their own agency towards the achievement of a goal. It is an individual exercising his or her relationship to what is around them in an instrumental way. Action without prior understanding, without prior inquiry, is likely to be chaotic and not goal-directed. Action towards others without respect will at best be patronizing and at worst, manipulative or authoritarian.

Although the skills outlined in Table 9.1 are those espoused in this work, it should be possible to translate the skills of any school of counselling or therapy into this model. Of course some schools may focus on some skills rather than others, but it is argued that unless that school can address the three levels in this model then in some sense it is failing to address the situation comprehensively.

The question now is what does this mean for family counselling?

The necessary and sufficient conditions

In 1957 Carl Rogers set himself a question. 'Is it possible to state, in terms which are clearly definable and measurable, the psychological conditions which are both necessary and sufficient to bring about constructive personality change?' (Rogers, 1957). His answer to his own question became a benchmark in the development of therapeutic and counselling practice. Perhaps now is the time to ask Rogers's question about constructive family systems change and whether we can specify the conditions 'necessary to initiate change' and 'sufficient to inaugurate the process'. There can be no better guidelines to this task than those outlined by Rogers himself. First, in following him we need to offer a definition of constructive change which for us involves the family system. Interestingly, in his 1957 definition of personality change, Rogers evokes the concept of objective observers agreeing about the change that takes place for the individual; the individual's own view is distinctly omitted. As we have seen, an observer influences any system and indeed the very concept of an objective observation is suspect. Therefore the client, that is the family, should be placed centre stage, and broadly following Rogers, the definition of constructive family systems change would read:

> Constructive family change involves change in the manner in which a family interacts with each other in a direction which the family agree means a greater ability to function in the dealing with life's tasks, that hence there is less dissatisfaction and conflict in their interaction and more energy utilizable for effective living enabling them to move towards developmental maturity.

Rogers then goes on to list several conditions of the change context.

1 That two persons are in relationship.
2 That the first, termed the client, is in a state of incongruence, being vulnerable or anxious.
3 That the second person, termed the therapist, is congruent or integrated in the relationship.
4 That the therapist experiences unconditional positive regard for the client.
5 That the therapist experiences an empathic understanding of the client's internal frame of reference.
6 That the communication to the client of the therapist's empathic understanding and unconditional positive regard is to a minimal degree achieved.

These conditions can be adapted for family systems change.

1 **A relationship must exist.** We have seen how human action is determined by the social context in which it occurs. Family systems change therefore can only occur within a relational context. For a considerable majority of time, change in families is the product of their own interaction. It is the product of their relationship. When a family confront difficulties, the introduction of a counsellor or therapist introduces a new web of relationships which can exist to facilitate the relationships already present. It is not necessary for the counsellor to have a relationship with every family member. His intervention into a part of the system connects him to the other parts and hence change becomes possible.

2 **Incongruence of the client.** Incongruence refers to a discrepancy between the actual experience of the individual and the self-picture of that individual insofar as it represents that experience. Not all family members will experience incongruence, as the usual situation is for some members to feel incongruent and believe that other family members are not understanding of and helpful towards this incongruence. Incongruence in some members is the experiential manifestation that a task posed for the family is not being dealt with adequately. Incongruence in families has often been discussed in terms of family satisfaction (see Olsen et al., 1984), incongruence in this case being the discrepancy between how family members perceived their family to be and their perception of their ideal version of the family. Families seeking help have been consistently shown to have greater discrepancy in this regard than those not seeking help.

3 **The counsellor/therapist is congruent in the relationship.** This means that within the relationship the counsellor is freely and deeply himself, with his experience accurately represented by his awareness of himself. This is obvious just for the period of the session. This means that the counsellor consciously interacts with the family in a way determined by himself and his choices of interaction and he does not allow himself to follow the family's preferences for interaction save where he determines to do so as a matter of conscious choice. The counsellor should be able to monitor his own actions and feelings so that he can detect when he is inappropriately reciprocating family interactions or introducing personal emotions, thoughts and behaviours which have no place in counselling this family. The counsellor should experience the feeling, 'I am freely able to attempt to interact in a way that I choose'.

4 **Unconditional positive regard.** Genuine interest in everybody and their voice in the family and a positive view of the members' potential as a family need to be present to make exploration possible. Sometimes family counsellors are required to meet families where there has been abuse, incest and similar extreme behaviours. By holding on to a systemic view which does not perceive a cause or place blame, it is possible to ask the question, 'How come things are like this?' in a way that implies non-judgemental acceptance, not of the individual behaviour but of the family context which produced that behaviour.

5 **Empathy.** In his discussion on empathy Rogers focuses on the therapist's experiencing an accurate understanding of the

individual's private world. When a family is being interviewed then clearly more than one individual is present. Therefore under this heading, two conditions can be proposed.

(a) The counsellor should experience an accurate empathic understanding of each individual's awareness of his or her own experience. Not only should the counsellor experience an appreciation of the perceptions and feelings of each individual but he should also experience a confidence that each person present has been allowed a voice.

(b) The counsellor should experience an understanding of the interactive process of the family. The interactive processes include the means by which the internal frames of reference of each family member interconnect as well as the interactive sequences that are present both in and outside of the counselling room.

6   **The communication of empathic understanding and unconditional positive regard**. This condition states that family members perceive the 'qualities' of the counsellor as he is able to communicate them through his interaction with the family. Again there are two elements that are important.

(a) The counsellor communicates his empathic understanding of each individual's experience. By this process family members have their own experience validated.

(b) The counsellor communicates his understanding of the interactive process of the family, such that each individual acquires an appreciation of their own and every other person's position in the systemic functioning of the family.

There does appear, however, to be another condition which is pertinent to family counselling and therapy, particularly as the counsellor is involved with interaction with more than one person. As we have seen in Chapter 4, the counsellor needs to be able to structure the sessions, particularly in the early stages, essentially so that conditions 3, 4, 5 and 6 can be seen in operation. The counsellor needs to create a social context in which each person is heard and feels heard and the counsellor's contribution can be appreciated by family members. Therefore it is proposed here that this also is a condition necessary and sufficient for family systems change.

7   **Setting the counselling context**. The counsellor should demonstrate the ability to create within the family and counsellor system the opportunity for each individual, including himself, to make their contribution to the functioning of that system.

As with Rogers's formulation for individual work, the concept being advanced here is that the essential conditions of change exist in a single configuration, even though counsellors may use them differentially, an implication being that the techniques of various schools are unimportant except to the extent that they serve as channels for fulfilling the conditions. The model of practice that has been advanced in this book is suggested as a means by which these conditions can be maximized. This method of outlining the core tasks of family counselling is a first step, perhaps the most important step, in being clear about what does and what does not work in offering therapy and counselling to families.

Using this set of conditions it may then be possible to attempt to define for family work another of Rogers's concepts, namely that of a 'molecule of therapeutic change' (Rogers, 1959). Indeed, this may well be based on family members' evaluations of the reflection sequences outlined in Chapter 3, for it is in these short sequences of interaction during the counselling process that difference becomes recognizable to the family and hence systems change can occur. Of course, different families and different types of problems may require different mixtures of the conditions and differing emphases to the skills outlined here. It will always be 'different strokes for different folks' but the importance of the conditions described above is that they represent the core elements from which different approaches can spring and perhaps they suggest where 'One' is for us as counsellors and therapists.

On becoming a family counsellor

Why is it that individuals seek to help others, and what needs to be done in order to do this? We each have an individual story that led us into helping others and we need to address those processes and issues in our stories that prevent us from being congruent with clients. I have elsewhere provided my story (Street, 1989) and readers will need to provide their own. Always at the beginning of our description of how we have come to be trying to do this kind of work will be the desire to help others but equally there remains a desire to understand ourselves. There is some realization that there is an element of being human that we do not quite have hold of and hence we must reach out for it. As Bateson (1973) has explained in his talk 'Consciousness and Nature', at any moment when we focus awareness on ourselves, on the 'me' and 'I', we limit our awareness of what is going on around us; we lose the sense of what we are connected to and what is connected to us. Such an individual personalized awareness only uses part of the mind and it is denying of nature to expect a part of the mind to understand its whole. Unfortunately, most of the time we settle for this very limited consciousness, but always the desire remains to expand that consciousness. We seek wisdom, that is, we seek knowledge of the larger interactive system of which we are a part.

How can we acquire this wisdom? Bateson offers three suggestions. First, we need to develop humility, both individually and societally. Secondly, we should expand our awareness and understanding of the systemic properties of the contexts we occupy. Thirdly, we should develop our creativity in art, poetry, religion, to which we can add the creativity of counselling and therapy. To become a counsellor you need to understand how you came to be doing it and the context of your doing of it. You need to learn the skills in this book. You should practise your creativity, then forget the skills in this book, forget your creativity, and with humility you can be your true self. As the old Zen saying goes, 'Thank you, master, for teaching me nothing'.

References

Andersen, T. (1987). The reflecting team: dialogue and meta-dialogue in clinical work. *Family Process*, 26: 415–28.

Anderson, C.M., Hogarty, G. and Reiss, D.J. (1985). *Schizophrenia in the Family: A Practitioner's Guide to Psychoeducation and Management*. New York: Guilford.

Auerswald, E.H. (1987). Epistemological confusion in family therapy and research. *Family Process*, 26: 317–30.

Bandler, R. and Grindler, J. (1975). *The Structure of Magic, 1*. Palo Alto, CA: Science and Behavior Books.

Bateson, G. (1973). *Steps to an Ecology of Mind*. St Albans: Paladin.

Bennun, I. (1989). Perceptions of the therapist in family therapy. *Journal of Family Therapy*, 11: 243–56.

Birdwhistell, R.L. (1959). *Contribution of Linguistic–Kinesic Studies to the Understanding of Schizophrenia: An Integrated Approach*. New York: Ronald Press.

Boszormenyi-Nagy, I. and Krasner, B.R. (1986). *Between Give and Take: A Clinical Guide to Contextual Therapy*. New York: Brunner/Mazel.

Bowen, M. (1978). *Family Therapy in Clinical Practice*. New York: Jason Aronson.

Brandon, D. (1983). Nowness in the helping relationship. In J. Welwood (ed.), *Awakening the Heart. East/West Approaches to Psychotherapy and the Healing Relationship*. Boston, MA: Shambala.

Breunlin, D.C. and Schwartz, R.C. (1986). Sequences: toward a common denominator of family therapy. *Family Process*, 25: 67–87.

Burnham, J. (1986). *Family Therapy*. London: Routledge.

Burnham, J. and Harris, Q. (1985). Therapy, supervision, consultation: different levels of a system. In D. Campbell and R. Draper (eds), *Applications of Systemic Therapy*. London: Grune and Stratton.

Byrne, E.A., Cunningham, C.C. and Sloper, P. (1988). *Families and Their Children with Down's Syndrome: One Feature in Common*. London: Routledge and Kegan Paul.

Cade, B. and Cornwell, M. (1985). New Realities for Old: Some Uses of Teams and One-Way Screens in Therapy. In D. Campbell and R. Draper (eds), *Applications of Systemic Family Therapy*. London: Grune and Stratton.

Campbell, D., Draper, R. and Huffington, C. (1989). *Second Thoughts on the Theory and Practice of the Milan Approach to Family Therapy*. London: Karnac.

Carpenter, J. and Treacher, A. (1989). *Problems and Solutions in Marital and Family Therapy*. Oxford: Basil Blackwell.

Carr, A. (1990). Failure in family therapy: a catalogue of engagement mistakes. *Journal of Family Therapy*, 12: 371–86.

Carter, B. and McGoldrick, M. (1989). Overview: the changing family life cycle. In B. Carter and M. McGoldrick (eds), *The Changing Family Life Cycle. A Framework for Family Therapy*, 2nd edn. Boston, MA: Allyn and Bacon.

Cecchin, G. (1987). Hypothesizing, circularity and neutrality revisited: an invitation to curiosity. *Family Process*, 26: 405–13.

Cecchin, G. (1988). Old wine in new bottles. Hypothesizing, neutrality and circularity revisited. *Association for Family Therapy Newsletter*, 8(4): 7–10.

Chase, J. and Holmes, J. (1990). Two year audit of a family therapy clinic in adult psychiatry. *Journal of Family Therapy*, 12: 229–42.

Cleghorn, J.M. and Levin, S. (1973). Training family therapists by setting learning objectives. *American Journal of Orthopsychiatry*, 43: 439–46.

Combrinck-Graham, L. (1981). Termination in family therapy. In A. Gurman (ed.), *Questions and Answers in the Practice of Family Therapy*. New York: Brunner/ Mazel.

Combrinck-Graham, L. (1985). A developmental model for family systems. *Family Process*, 24: 139–50.

Conyne, R.K. and O'Neil, J.M. (eds) (1992). *Organizational Consultation: A Casebook*. London: Sage.

Crane, D.R., Griffin, W. and Hill, R.D. (1986). Influence of therapist skills on client perceptions of marriage and family therapy outcome: implications for supervision. *Journal of Marital and Family Therapy*, 12: 91–6.

Cronen, V.E. and Pearce, W.B. (1985). Towards an explanation of how the Milan Method works: an invitation to a systemic epistemology and the evolution of family systems. In D. Campbell and R. Draper (eds), *Applications of Systemic Family Therapy: the Milan Approach*. London: Grune and Straton.

Crook, J.H. (1980). *The Evolution of Human Consciousness*. Oxford: Clarendon Press.

Crowther, C., Dare, C. and Wilson, J. (1990). 'Why should we talk to you? You'll only tell the Court!' On being an informer and a family therapist. *Journal of Family Therapy*, 12: 105–22.

Dallos, R. (1991). *Family Belief Systems, Therapy and Change*. Milton Keynes: Open University Press.

Dammann, C. (1984). Private practice. In M. Berger and G.J. Jarkovic (eds), *Practicing Family Therapy in Diverse Settings*. San Francisco, CA: Jossey Bass.

Dare, C. and Lindsey, C. (1979). Children in Family Therapy. *Journal of Family Therapy*, 1: 253–69.

DeShazer, S. (1982). *Patterns of Brief Family Therapy: an Ecosystemic Approach*. New York: Guilford.

Dimmock, B. and Dungworth, D. (1983). Creating manoeuvrability for family/ systems therapists in social services departments. *Journal of Family Therapy*, 5: 53–69.

Doherty, W.J. and Colangelo, N. (1984). The Family FIRO Model: a modest proposal for organizing family treatment. *Journal of Marital and Family Therapy*, 10: 19–29.

Doherty, W.J., Colangelo, N. and Hovander, D. (1991). Priority setting in family change and clinical practice: the FIRO Model. *Family Process*, 30: 227–40.

Dowling, E. (1993). Are family therapists listening to the young? A psychological perspective. *Journal of Family Therapy*, 15: 403–12.

Egan, G. (1990). *The Skilled Helper: a Systemic Approach to Effective Helping*, 4th edn. Pacific Grove, CA: Brooks/Cole.

Epston, D. and White, M. (1989). *Literate Means to Therapeutic Ends*. Adelaide: Dulwich Centre Publications.

Folkman, S. (1984). Personal control and stress and coping processes: A theoretical analysis. *Journal of Personality and Social Psychology*, 48: 839–52.

Folkman, S. and Lazarus, R.S. (1980). An analysis of coping in a middle-aged community sample. *Journal of Health and Social Behaviour*, 21: 219–39.

Folkman, S. and Lazarus, R.S. (1985). If it changes, it must be process: a study of emotion and coping during three stages of a college examination. *Journal of Personality and Social Psychology*, 48: 150–70.

Gilhooly, M.L.M. (1987). Senile dementia and the family. In J. Orford (ed.), *Coping with Disorder in the Family*. London: Croom Helm.

Goldberg, C.D.S. and David, A.S. (1991). Family therapy and the glamour of science. *Journal of Family Therapy*, 12: 17–29.

Green, R.J. and Herget, M. (1991). Outcomes of systemic/strategic team consultation. III: The importance of therapist warmth and active structuring. *Family Process*, 30: 321–36.

Greenberg, L.S. (1991). Research on the process of change. *Psychotherapy Research*, 1: 3–16.

Gurman, A.S. (1983). Family therapy research and the new epistemology. *Journal of Marital and Family Therapy*, 9: 227–34.

Gurman, A.S. and Kniskern, D.P. (1981). Family therapy outcome research: knowns and unknowns. In A.S. Gurman and D.P. Kniskern (eds), *Handbook of Family Therapy*. New York: Brunner/Mazel.

Gurman, A.S., Kniskern, D. and Pinsof, W. (1985). Research on the process and outcome of marital and family therapy. In S. Garfield and A. Bergin (eds), *Handbook of Psychotherapy and Behaviour Change*, 3rd edn. New York: Wiley.

Hardwick, P.J. (1991). Families and the professional network: an attempted classification of professional network actions which can hinder change. *Journal of Family Therapy*, 13: 187–205.

Hawkins, P. and Shohet, R. (1989). *Supervision in the Helping Profession*. Milton Keynes: Open University Press.

Haley, J. (1976). *Problem Solving Therapy*. New York: Harper and Row.

Heath, A. (1985). Ending family therapy – some new directions. *Family Therapy Collections*, 14: 33–40.

Hetherington, E.M. and Clingempeel, W.G. (1992). Coping with marital transitions: a family systems perspective. *Monographs of the Society for Research in Child Development*, 57(2–3).

Heubeck, B., Watson, J. and Russell, G. (1986). Father involvement and responsibility in family therapy. In M. Lamb (ed.), *The Father's Role: Applied Perspectives*. New York: Wiley.

Hoffman, L. (1985). Beyond power and control: toward a 'second order' family systems therapy. *Family Systems Medicine*, 3: 381–96.

Hoffman, L. (1989). The family life cycle and discontinuous change. In B. Carter and M. McGoldrick (eds), *The Changing Family Life Cycle: A Framework for Family Therapy*, 2nd edn. Boston, MA: Allyn and Bacon.

Hora, T. (1983). Asking the right question. In J. Welwood (ed.), *Awakening the Heart*. Boston, MA: Shambala.

Jacobson, N.S. and Margolin, G. (1979). *Marital Therapy*. New York: Brenner/Mazel.

Kelly, G.A. (1955). *The Psychology of Personal Constructs*. New York: Norton.

Kingston, P. (1984). 'But they aren't motivated . . .': issues concerned with encouraging motivation for change in families. *Journal of Family Therapy*, 6: 381–403.

Kingston, P. and Smith, D. (1983). Preparation for live consultation and live supervision when working without a one-way screen. *Journal of Family Therapy*, 5: 219–33.

Knussen, C. and Sloper, P. (1992). Stress in families of children with disability: a review of risk and resistance factors. *Journal of Mental Health*, 1: 241–56.

Lazarus, R.S. (1990). Theory-based stress measurement. *Psychological Inquiry*, 1: 3–13.

Lewis, J.M. (1986). Family structure and stress. *Family Process*, 25: 235–47.

Minuchin, S. (1974). *Families and Family Therapy*. London: Tavistock.

Napier, A.Y. and Whitaker, C.A. (1978). *The Family Crucible*. New York: Harper and Row.

McGoldrick, M., Pearce, J.K. and Giordano, J. (eds) (1982). *Ethnicity and Family Therapy*. New York: Guilford.

Nichols, M.R. (1987). *The Self in the System: Expanding the Limits of Family Therapy*. New York: Brunner/Mazel.

O'Brien, A. and Loudon, P. (1985). Redressing the balance – involving children in family therapy. *Journal of Family Therapy*, 7: 81–98.

Olsen, D.H., McCubbin, H.I., Barnes, M., Larsen, A., Muxen, M. and Wilson, M. (1984). *Families: What Makes Them Work?* Beverly Hills, CA: Sage.

Olsen, D.H., Russell, C.S. and Sprenkle, D.H. (eds) (1988). *Circumplex Model: Systemic Assessment and Treatment of Families*. New York: Haworth Press.

O'Reilly, P. and Street, E. (1988). Experiencing the past in the present: a historical approach to family therapy. In E. Street and W. Dryden (eds), *Family Therapy in Britain*. Milton Keynes: Open University Press.

Palazzoli, M., Boscolo, L., Cecchin, G. and Pratsa, G. (1980a). Hypothesizing – circularity – neutrality: three guidelines for the conductor of a session. *Family Process*, 19: 3–12.

Palazzoli, M., Boscolo, L., Cecchin, G. and Prata, G. (1980b). The problem of the referring person. *Journal of Marital and Family Therapy*, 6: 3–9.

Palazzoli, M.S., Cecchin, G., Prata, G. and Boscolo, L. (1978). *Paradox and Counterparadox*. New York: Jason Aronson.

Pearce, W.B. and Cronen, V.E. (1980). *Communication, Action and Meaning: The Creation of Social Realities*. New York: Praeger.

Perls, F.S., Hefferkubem R.P. and Goodman, P. (1973). *Gestalt Therapy*. Harmondsworth: Penguin Books.

Perelberg, R.J. and Miller, A.C. (eds) (1990). *Gender and Power in Families*. London: Routledge.

Pimpernell, P. and Treacher, A. (1990). Using a videotape to overcome client reluctance to engage in family therapy – some preliminary findings from a probation setting. *Journal of Family Therapy*, 12: 59–72.

Pinsof, W.M. (1981). Family therapy process research. In A.S. Gurman and D.P. Kniskern (eds), *Handbook of Family Therapy*. New York: Brunner/Mazel.

Pinsof, W.M. (1983). Integrative problem-centered therapy: toward the synthesis of family and individual psychotherapies. *Journal of Marital and Family Therapy*, 9: 19–35.

Raskin, N.J. and Van der Veen, F. (1970). Client-centered family therapy: some clinical and research perspectives. In J.T. Hart and T.M. Tomlinson (eds), *New Directions in Client-Centered Therapy*. Boston, MA: Houghton Mifflin.

Reder, P. and Kraemer, S. (1980). Dynamic aspects of professional collaboration in child guidance referral. *Journal of Adolescence*, 3: 165–73.

Robinson, M. (1991). *Family Transformation through Divorce and Remarriage*. London: Routledge.

Rogers, C. (1951). *Client Centered Therapy*. Boston, MA: Houghton Mifflin.

Rogers, C. (1957). The necessary and sufficient conditions for therapeutic personality change. *Journal of Consulting Psychology*, 21: 95–103.

Rogers, C.R. (1959). The essence of psychotherapy: a client centered view. *Annals of Psychotherapy*, 1: 51–7.

Rogers, C.R. (1967). *On Becoming a Person*. London: Constable.

Rolland, J.S. (1984). A psychosocial typology of chronic illness. *Family Systems Medicine*, 2: 245–62.

Rolland, J.S. (1987). Chronic illness and the life cycle: a conceptual framework. *Family Process*, 26: 203–21.

Rutter, M. (1987). Psychosocial resilience and protective mechanisms. In S. Rolk, A. Master, D. Cicchetti, K. Muechterlein and S. Weintraub (eds), *Risk and Protection Factors in the Development of Psychopathology*. New York: Cambridge University Press.

Schafer, R. (1959). Generative empathy in the treatment situation. *Psychoanalytic Quarterly*, 28: 342–73.

Schutz, W.C. (1966). *The Interpersonal World*. Palo Alto, CA: Science and Behavior Books.

Sokolov, I. and Hutton, D. (1988). *The Parents Book: Getting on Well With Our Children*. Wellingborough: Thorsons.

Speed, B., Seligman, P., Kingston, P. and Cade, B. (1982). A team approach to therapy. *Journal of Family Therapy*, 4: 271–84.

Street, E. (1985). From child-focused problems to marital issues. In W. Dryden (ed.), *Marital Therapy in Britain*, vol. 2: *Special Areas*. London: Harper and Row.

Street, E. (1988). Family therapy training research: systems model and review. *Journal of Family Therapy*, 10: 383–402.

Street, E. (1989). Challenging the 'White Knight'. In W. Dryden and L. Spurling (eds), *On Becoming a Psychotherapist*. London: Tavistock/Routledge.

Street, E., Downey, J. and Brazier, A. (1991). The development of therapeutic consultations in child-focused family work. *Journal of Family Therapy*, 13: 311–34.

Street, E. and Reimers, S. (1993). Family therapy services for children. In J. Carpenter and A. Treacher (eds), *Using Family Therapy in the 90s*. Oxford: Basil Blackwell.

Terkelsen, K.G. (1980). Toward a theory of the family life cycle. In B. Carter and M. McGoldrick (eds), *The Family Life Cycle*. New York: Gardner Press.

Todd, T.C. (1984). Family therapist as administrator: roles and responsibilities. M. Berger and G.J. Jurkovic (eds), *Practicing Family Therapy in Diverse Settings*. San Francisco: Jossey-Bass.

Tomm, K. (1985). Circular interviewing: a multifaceted clinical tool. In D. Campbell and R. Draper (eds), *Applications of Systemic Family Therapy*. London: Grune and Stratton.

Tomm, K. (1987). Interventive interviewing: part II. Reflexive questioning as a means to enable self-healing. *Family Process*, 26: 167–83.

Tomm, K. (1988). Interventive interviewing: part III. Intending to ask lineal, circular, strategic or reflexive questions. *Family Process*, 27: 1–15.

Tomm, K. and Wright, L.M. (1979). Family therapy skills. *Family Process*, 18: 227–50.

Treacher, A. (1989). Termination in family therapy – developing a structural approach. *Journal of Family Therapy*, 11: 135–48.

Watzlawick, P., Weakland, J. and Fisch, R. (1974). *Change: Principles of Problem Formation and Problem Resolution*. New York: Norton.

Weakland, J.H. and Jordan, L. (1992). Working briefly with reluctant clients: child protective services as an example. *Journal of Family Therapy*, 14: 231–54.

Welwood, J. (1983). Befriending emotion. In J. Welwood (ed.), *Awakening the Heart*. Boston, MA: Shambala.

Whitaker, C.A. and Keith, D.U. (1981). Symbolic-experiential family therapy. In A.S. Gurman and D.P. Knickern (eds), *Handbook of Family Therapy*. New York: Brunner/Mazel.

Wilkinson, M. (1992). How do we understand empathy systemically? *Journal of Family Therapy*, 14: 193–206.

Wolberg, L.R. (1980). *Handbook of Short-Term Psychotherapy*. New York: Thieme-Stratton.

Wynne, L.C. (1984). The epigenesis of relational systems: a model for understanding family development. *Family Process*, 23: 297–318.

Index